"In this current time, when the tendency is to remain in a comfortable, like-minded cultural silo, . . . Bob invites his readers to explore the gray area of hard questions and encourages critical thinking about ideas of faith, belief, and community. He does this in a care-filled way that steers clear of judgement and offers a path to understanding that communities of faith are made stronger when approached, challenged, and understood thoughtfully."

—K<small>RISTEN</small> G<small>RAVES</small>,
singer/songwriter

"Prophetic and yet loving. Appreciative and yet challenging. Written with a pastor's heart and an academic mind, this text invites pastors and congregational leaders to ponder how they can be more faithful to the gospel in our time. In a time of apparent decline, this text provides images of hope for a vital church of the future. A great book for group study as well as personal reflection. I commend it for church-leadership teams and councils."

—Bruce Epperly,
author of *Walking with Francis of Assisi: From Privilege to Activism*

"LaRochelle delivers a personal Jacob-wrestling-with-the-angel story. . . . This honest confessional by one who has served as a pastor in multiple congregations of various denominations is a candid look at what the local church can become if its priorities are rooted in a sense of mission and discipleship."

—James Hazelwood,
author of *Everyday Spirituality: Discover a Life of Hope, Meaning and Peace*

"LaRochelle points to both the excesses and shortcomings of the hierarchical, rule-based structure of the church while also pointing to the fact that much of humanitarian assistance comes from faith-based organizations. He . . . challenges the church to become more relevant and directly address the current challenges facing its congregants."

—Curtis Brand,
author of *Butterfly Moon*

"LaRochelle offers us a refreshingly honest glimpse into his lifelong relationship with the church and the internal conflict that helped to shape his journey. . . . This book is a perfect conversation starter as the reader explores their own personal relationship with God, religion, and the church."

—Eric R. Hutchinson,
Music Director, Grace Lutheran Church, ELCA

"In reading this book, I found myself reenergized as a Christian. It answered deep-rooted questions about the purpose of the church and what could be as opposed to its current realities. In many ways, I view this book as a call to action. . . . What are our priorities? What should they be? This book is timely and has the opportunity to serve as a catalyst for both personal and institutional change."

—DANIEL P. SULLIVAN III,
Connecticut School Administrator

"LaRochelle looks back on his lifework 'navigating life within the institutional church.' . . . What sets LaRochelle's work apart is its pastoral focus, setting these large questions within the context of local pastoral life. Doing so . . . offers hope that solutions can be found that will renew Christian care in the Christian movement's many intersecting American communities."

—DAVID O BRIEN,
author of *The Renewal of American Catholicism*

"LaRochelle speaks for many clergy when he writes about his love-hate relationship with the church. . . . We have a book that explores the values and the challenges of the church, resulting in this love-hate relationship. As a mainline pastor (now retired), I recognize the realities described here. My hope is that readers will discern from the book a path forward so that the good news can be experienced by all who encounter the church."

—ROBERT CORNWALL,
author of *Called to Bless*

"LaRochelle clearly has a true love for the church. And as with any true love, he's committed to making it work. But he is not blinded by its trappings, nor its dangers. Bob doesn't see the church just in static absolutes but rather with the nuance that is necessary for the church's survival and to reach its maximum positive impact in our society—and in ourselves. During these times, thinking like this is exactly what we need."

—BRYAN NURNBERGER,
President & Founder, Simply Smiles

I Love the Church,
I Hate the Church

I Love the Church,
I Hate the Church

Paradox or Contradiction?

ROBERT R. LAROCHELLE

RESOURCE *Publications* • Eugene, Oregon

I LOVE THE CHURCH, I HATE THE CHURCH
Paradox or Contradiction?

Copyright © 2022 Robert R. LaRochelle. All rights reserved. Except for brief quotations in critical publications or reviews, no part of this book may be reproduced in any manner without prior written permission from the publisher. Write: Permissions, Wipf and Stock Publishers, 199 W. 8th Ave., Suite 3, Eugene, OR 97401.

Resource Publications
An Imprint of Wipf and Stock Publishers
199 W. 8th Ave., Suite 3
Eugene, OR 97401

www.wipfandstock.com

PAPERBACK ISBN: 978-1-6667-1384-8
HARDCOVER ISBN: 978-1-6667-1385-5
EBOOK ISBN: 978-1-6667-1386-2

JANUARY 25, 2022 8:42 AM

This book is dedicated to my wife Patricia
with deep gratitude for her love and support.

Contents

Introduction	Why This Book?	1
1	Hating What I Love	11
2	Where There Is Hatred, Love	31
3	The Local Church	47
4	Church: Social Club or Community of Disciples?	64
5	The Crisis of Church Documents	79
6	We Have Always Done It that Way	88
7	The Church as Countercultural	101
8	Do We Need the Church?	109
9	Before We Conclude …	118
10	In Conclusion	128

Bibliography | 133

Introduction

WHY THIS BOOK?

IN THE INTEREST OF FULL DISCLOSURE, I would like to begin by saying that I struggled with my decision to give this book the title I eventually chose. As I considered my options, I could not help but think that by calling the book *I Love the Church, I Hate the Church: Paradox or Contradiction?* I was conveying some inaccurate impressions to you, the reader. After all, as you will see in reading it, religious faith has been an important part of my life and I did not want you to think that my intention was to engage in a vitriolic critique of faith and its place in so many peoples' hearts. As I think you will see as you read this book, my faith means a lot to me and using the word *hate* to describe it in any way is something that most certainly does not come easily. Nevertheless, that title had an appeal to me because it most certainly does express the deeply rooted and conflicting emotions I have formed over many decades of navigating life within the institutional church as both a member and a leader.

As I seek to be honest and transparent with you, the reader, I can freely admit that in the years I have spent growing up in the church and then eventually opting to be an ordained leader within it, I most certainly have developed a disdain for many of its practices. It is important that I let you know something about my background. As you read this book and inevitably learn more about me, you will most likely notice that, despite my many concerns and complaints or maybe *because* of them, I am an individual for whom institutional religion has had a very significant place in my life for a very long time. I detail this experience in depth in a previous book I have written entitled *Crossing the Street*[1]. While that book goes into detail about the differences to be found between Catholicism and Protestantism, it does so within the context of my decision to leave the Roman Catholic Church in 1998, a very significant decision in my life.

However, my experience in the world of Protestant Christianity has reinforced for me what I knew on some level when I made the decision to leave the church of my youth. In retrospect, I can see that through living and serving in both Catholic and Protestant circles, I have come to the clear recognition that I have really struggled with so much that I have seen and experienced within organized religion, whether it be Protestant or Catholic. Through the years, I have become quite aware of the levels of emotion I have felt quite intensely as I have dealt with a multiplicity of issues related to the institutional churches of which I have been a part. As I developed this book that you have in your hands (or on your computer screen) right now, I realized that it was important to share some personal information with you as you begin the process of reading it and, along the way, I would hope, reflecting upon your own experience of religious faith within your life, an experience that is unique to everyone reading this book.

I think it is important that you are aware of this: I was raised as a very active Roman Catholic boy and young man. I began serving as an altar boy for a group of sisters (popularly known as nuns)when I was nine years old and I continued doing so right through my high school years. I spent an awful lot of time throughout those years considering entering the Roman Catholic priesthood but ultimately never took that step. Having attended a Roman Catholic college run by the Jesuits[2], I soon thereafter embarked on what would become a career in Catholic education. Along the way, I completed a master's degree in the field of religious education from yet another Jesuit college[3] and then proceeded to settle into a daily routine of teaching religion to students in Catholic high schools.

While doing that, in addition to my work within those schools throughout many years as both a teacher and counselor as well as a baseball and basketball coach, I was also active in several local Catholic parishes. This included taking on the responsibilities of serving in various professional positions within them, including leading youth ministry programs

---

1. LaRochelle, *Crossing the Street*

2. My undergraduate degree is from the College of the Holy Cross, an institution run by the Jesuits, whose formal title is the Society of Jesus.

3. Boston College, Chestnut Hill, Massachusetts.

Why This Book?

as well as directing retreats for adolescents and serving as a director of religious education in three different Catholic churches. While over the course of this time I had lowered any expectations that I might one day enter the Catholic priesthood, I did set my eyes on a possible goal for when I eventually would reach the age of 35.

As I drew closer to that age, I began the process of applying to enter the four-year permanent diaconate program of the Roman Catholic Archdiocese of Hartford, Connecticut. Within the Catholic Church, the permanent diaconate is an ordained ministry, as is the case with the better-known Catholic priesthood. I saw the diaconate as a ministry to which Catholic married men such as I could aspire. As a deacon, I could preach, baptize, preside at prayer services in the local parish, proclaim the Gospel at Mass and officiate at funerals and burials as needed. I would be remiss were I not to say that the fact that it was open only to *men* is something I found deeply disturbing, yet I had concluded at that point in my life that it was a viable way for me to be of service and that service would include activity in the church which might really be of help to individuals often troubled by the ways in which they were mistreated by this institution. I was once challenged by a very bright and dedicated Catholic woman who argued that if men really wanted to see progress on behalf of women within Catholicism what they needed to do is stop entering programs preparing them for ordination, something denied to women. She raised a very good point! While I maintained that, despite some policies I considered inadequate, the community of the church needed priests and deacons, I have never forgotten the deep wisdom inherent in her challenging remark. In fact, I see it as a message that might very well need to be heard within the current context of Roman Catholicism. After all, many years removed from my conversation with this woman, the fact remains that only men are eligible for ordination in the Roman Catholic Church, something I consider quite problematic!

Consequently, however, in my years as an ordained Catholic clergyperson serving in the permanent diaconate, I found myself centered on conveying a message to fellow Catholics that, despite many of the obstacles put up by Catholic hierarchies that had found their way into official church teachings and policies, at its core Catholicism was about communicating what Jesus of Nazareth was all about and providing individuals with practical opportunities to put this faith in Jesus into practice. Along the way, many people expressed appreciation for the ways in which I conveyed the Catholic expression of Christian faith to them. Through my years as a deacon, I also faced some pushback from more traditionalist Catholics who were not comfortable with some things I said in my homilies[4] which they considered to be too liberal. My position was always that what got the church started in the first place and what remained its driving force was its focus on the teachings of Jesus, as seen within the context of the experience of what we call Easter. *It was quite clear to me that were one to take the teachings of Jesus seriously, one would see how challenging they are because of the ways in which they confronted the social order and religious practices of his day.* I am most grateful that both in my Jesuit education and back in my high school days when I was fortunate enough to have been taught by a wonderful young priest[5], my teachers conveyed to me the importance of reading the life of Jesus in relation to the early church's experience of resurrection. This entailed an approach to reading the Gospels which one could call *reading backwards*. By this I mean that one recognizes that the very reason these Gospel writings ever existed had to do with the experience of the Resurrection. Consequently, what Jesus did and said should be read within this broader context. *Somewhere along the line I began to understand that it was the belief among many followers that Jesus, once crucified, was still very much alive that formed the core of my faith.* To be clear, this is not a contention that Jesus, who once lived in Nazareth, is hanging out somewhere in Chicago or in Boise, Idaho.

Instead, it is a belief expressed in the beautiful and gripping words of Gerard Manley Hopkins, a distinguished poet who also happened to be a Jesuit priest:

> *For I say this: The just man justices, keeps grace that keeps all his goings graces acts in God's eyes what in God's eyes he is: Christ!*
> *For Christ plays in ten thousand places, lovely in limbs and lovely eyes not his, plays to the Father through the features of men's faces*[6].

I felt that the message I had shared for years with teenagers both in the classroom and on retreats was one that anyone whom I knew who was connected to Catholicism in any way needed to hear as well. It was a simple message: Christianity is centered on the way of life espoused by Jesus and expressed in what He said and how He lived! The institutional

---

4. A term used within Catholicism to describe the preached message within the worship service. In Protestant tradition, this is best known as a sermon.

5. Father William Fogarty of the Marian Fathers, who died at the all too young age of 39.

6. Hopkins, *As Kingfishers Catch Fire*.

church, I thought, oftentimes messed this important message up with its emphasis on rules, policies, and specific church laws. I came to believe this even though I realized that one could not function as an institution without some laws. Nonetheless, I saw a significant distinction between reasonable law and the problems attached to legalism.

Now, truth be told, in those years when I served as a Catholic deacon, while I loved conveying the message about Jesus that I have just described, there were many things about the way the institution of the church ran that, to be honest, I really despised. This included everything from rules and policies related to annulments[7], the church's denial of Communion to those in invalid marriages, to an unreasonable approach to issues related to birth control, as well as the church's continued inability to function with the recognition that it is healthy and sensible to espouse a separation of church and state. As I concluded the writing of this book, I read a story on my Twitter account regarding how a priest asked a student in a Catholic school to take off her gay pride shirt as she attended Mass[8]. The presence and proliferation of stories such as these over the years have been truly disturbing to me. On an emotional level as well as the level of honest thought, I have *despised* many of the impediments the institutional church has put in the way of what I understood the Gospel of Jesus to be about. However, before you read any further, I need you to know something very important: *Though you will read about the why and the how of my leaving the Catholic Church and becoming a Protestant, I don't want you thinking that I am anti Catholic in any way, shape, or form.* In fact, despite the issues I may have had (and still do) with some policies and aspects of the church's theology, I am *profoundly grateful* for my Catholic upbringing and education. In addition, even as I lead worship in Protestant congregations, I continue to be influenced by Catholic spirituality, which I often experience as I preside at worship services in Protestant churches.

However, in the earliest period of my college experience, I had begun to be fascinated with a side of Christianity of which I never saw much in my early formation as a Roman Catholic young man. As a student at Holy Cross, I began reading significant books and other writings authored by

---

7. An annulment is a declaration of nullity regarding a marriage. If one receives an annulment, one is free to remarry within the Catholic Church if the prospective spouse has no impediment to marriage. Over the course of my ministry as a deacon, I helped many individuals who were seeking annulments.

8. This took place at St. Francis of Assisi school and parish in Northeast Baltimore, Maryland.

well-known Protestant theologians and thinkers. I took it upon myself to spend time every weekend participating in both the Catholic worship service (Mass) on campus and then, on most of my weekends during the academic year, going off campus and attending a church of some Protestant denomination in my college's hometown of Worcester, Massachusetts. Inevitably, when I did so, I also asked if I could have a meeting with the pastor so I could ask him[9] some questions or I would show up at one of the church sponsored Sunday morning educational forums. These experiences of searching and of learning were very formative ones for me. I appreciated the opportunity to connect the experiences of worship that had become part of my life with the fascinating theological writings to which I was being exposed regularly. For a variety of reasons, I took a particular liking to Martin Luther. I was most fortunate to have been taught in two of my classes at Holy Cross by a distinguished Lutheran theologian[10]. In those classes, we both read a lot about Luther and explored his teachings in considerable detail. When reflecting on why that interest in Luther might be so significant to me, I came to realize that it was his own struggle with the Catholicism around which he centered his life that resonated with my own experience. I also found him to be a fascinating writer and someone who, despite his great intellectual depth, really knew how to lay his heart on the line as he addressed a plethora of important questions and issues that played out in the culture of his day. I perceived him as a person who was amazingly self-aware of the complexities of being human and discovered that even when I thought he had gone off the rails with some of his ideas and biases, this was a man who was really trying hard to live a good life and who most definitively embraced the value and depth of who Jesus was and what he taught! I found myself enjoying the process of reading many of his voluminous works.

I could go on and on about the internal questioning and agitation that I experienced over the course of many years, both in my undergraduate days and well beyond. As I noted above, I describe this in considerable detail in my book *Crossing the Street* which I have cited previously. I hope you may consider reading about it as a complement to this book you are reading right here and now. Yet, to cut to the chase, I will just tell you that, after experiencing much internal deliberation and anguish, I decided, at the age

---

9. Unfortunately, in the early 1970's, there were not many women clergy around in the areas in which I grew up and went to college.

10. Dr. Dennis Ormseth

Why This Book?

of 45, to leave the church of my youth and my early to middle adulthood and to become a Protestant and also to pursue the possibility of eventually serving as an ordained clergyperson within the Protestant branch of what I believed to be the universal catholic[11]church, *a church in which Protestants, Catholic and Orthodox, despite doctrinal differences, are united in a common faith, centered in Jesus of Nazareth.*

Now, in writing this introduction, I have tried to present you with a description of the fact that I have had considerable internal struggles with this institution we call church. You will get some of the details about a good number of these struggles as you read the following pages. As a result of them, I find that it is straightforward and honest to say that *while I most certainly do not hate the church, in the sense of wishing it ill, yes, I nonetheless do have an ambivalent relationship with the church as an institution.* There is an awful lot about the institutional church that bothers me and stirs up some powerful emotions! I believe that, in every age, the church needs to be open to reform and conversant with the signs of the times. It is obvious to me that it has not always been such and I find that fact most troubling!

To be clear, this *hatred* is a form of *disgust* that an institution, built on the incredible teachings and amazing life of Jesus, could put up such barriers that would impede individuals from understanding the core principles of Jesus' life and how those principles could influence their lives and, through them, the broader world. What you will see in this book is my profound disdain for what I describe as a *legalism* within the church which has had so deleterious an effect both internally and in the eyes of those who are looking at the church from the outside, oftentimes thinking that's as far as they would ever want to go and eventually would decide that they never want to take the step and enter. This is best defined as a focus on necessary rules and regulations without a concurrent understanding of the situations and circumstances involved in the decision-making process of the individual faced with often complex ethical choices.

Now, traditionalist Christians of all stripes might find this last statement of mine to be quite problematic. They might say that my thinking is influenced by an unhealthy sense of relativism and a denial of anything that is absolute. Traditional Catholics would cite church teachings and practices surrounding issues such as birth control, annulments, homosexuality, and

---

11. Catholic with a small 'c' refers to the 'universal' church, not specifically the Roman Catholic church. Consequently, many Protestant churches profess the Creed at worship which alludes to "one, holy, catholic, and apostolic" church.

many more in terms of understanding what they would see cite as the natural law as established by God, from their perspective. *I would disagree with their analysis.* As I hope is clear in this brief introduction, I am passionate about the teachings of Jesus, yet I also know that any institution which operates within a particular culture is susceptible, in some sense, to being led by the values and practices of the culture or, in the case of the church, by approaches to church teaching or physical structure[12] that developed at a particular time in history and have remained as fixed teachings, established practice and, in many cases, standard church architecture. My hope is that in a later chapter, I will be able to spell that out in a way that adequately describes what I mean when I write that.

As you go through these upcoming pages, I hope that you will find yourself entering a conversation with this book and with others who are reading it as well. *In fact, I also would love it if this short piece of writing would be used by people in local churches as a means for examining their own practices and traditions.* I would be quite excited to know that this book is being used in adult education programs within congregations! This process of examination might very well lead readers in the direction of practical questions not only as to what works in terms of a church considering itself to be successful, but rather deeper ones concerning what the church really ought to be about. In addition, as I think you will see in the future pages you will read, when I think of or when I am asked what the church needs at this period in its history, I immediately respond by claiming that churches really need intense self-examination as to their primary purpose and how to put that purpose into practical effect.

With all of that in mind, here is a brief outline and overview of what you are about to read:

In the first chapter, I write about *hating what I love.* In this chapter, you may find me quite critical about the ways in which local church practices are shaped by a sense of the way things always were. You will also find here a sympathetic interpretation of the word *hate* as used within that context. Building on this foundation, Chapter 2 takes its title from the prayer of Francis of Assisi, *a prayer that expresses a need for hate to be replaced by love.* This chapter explores the ambivalence in the relationship one might

---

12. The architecture of most Catholic churches in the United States, for example, was modeled on the churches found in major centers of the European Continent. In saying this, I also would note the practice of placing the altar well in the front with members of the congregation viewing from afar. I describe this as a vertical approach to worship. I write more about this later in this book.

Why This Book?

have with a church that functions both as community and as an institution at one and the same time.

Chapter 3 gets into nitty gritty detail about the *local church*. In this chapter, we look at typical church dynamics and what people often call *the politics* inherent in church life. Building on this, in Chapter 4 we raise the question of church function. We explore the church as being either a social club or a *community of disciples*. Chapter 5 addresses what I call *the crisis of church documents* as I seek to unveil what often drives the constitutions and by laws of local churches, the influence of a culture outside of Christian community inherent in them, as well as look at some of their all too often hidden strengths. In addition, this chapter takes us inside some typical practices often found in more traditional models of local church governance. In this analysis, I also seek to draw some distinctions concerning how different kinds of churches may approach these matters differently.

Chapter 6 is centered on one of my pet peeves as a church member and as a pastor. This chapter centers on the notion that churches find solace in the ways they have always done things which have since morphed into traditions which have been well established. My goal is that this be a serious exploration of the good and the bad of traditions as lived out in the local church. Chapter 7 is highly influenced by the writings of H. Richard Niebuhr and some others. In it, I cite one of my favorite books[13], which I identify as a helpful guide in exploring questions regarding what a church should strive to be. The title of this chapter is a simple and direct one pointing us in the direction of exploring the countercultural nature of the church. Chapter 8 raises the question *of whether we need the church* with the inspiration for that question drawn from a book by that name from one of my favorite professors from my early graduate school days. In this chapter, I will attempt to explain my conviction that this question, in and of itself, is a necessary one for people connected with the church to ask. In Chapter 9, I veer off into some theological reflection as I seek to explore the various ways that people understand what they mean when they say or otherwise use the word *God*. I think this exploration of theological diversity is extremely important in understanding the pluralism found in the institutional church as well as among those who self-identify as Christians.

Chapter 10, our concluding chapter, is my attempt to take the topics I have written about in prior chapters and offer practical suggestions in response to significant points of emphasis made in them.

13. Niebuhr, *Christ and Culture*

A final and extremely important note before we move forward into the heart of this book:

As you may have noticed, the title of the book acknowledges that this love/hate relationship of the author to the institutional church might very well be either a paradox and contradiction or both. This is an important distinction. While the title may be perceived as contradictory and that is understandable, the word paradox provides a fuller clarification of what I am trying to say through these words. *In essence, what I am attempting to express is that there is an awful lot within institutional religion that I truly despise and hate, while at the very same time, there is so, so much that I love deeply and dearly.* Those looking for a book which will tear down the faith known as Christianity will not find it here! As you read this book, I ask that you reflect carefully upon this crucial distinction. I have not written this book to tear down organized religion. Conversely, I have written it with a desire to be straightforward, honest and, where need be, critical with the core inspiration for those critiques being a deeply seated love of that institution I criticize! *While the emotions involved in both loving and hating may seem to many to be contradictory, I see them as paradoxical instead, i.e., an apparent contradiction that really is not!*

It is my sincere hope that, in your reading, you will find in the experiences I have shared some that may resonate with your own. Whether that happens or not, I hope that you will find in this book some important questions for reflection on where the church fits into your life or whether it even fits in at all. At times you may catch yourself wondering why I am so critical of so many aspects of life in the institution we call church. At other times, you may ask that if I am this critical, why would I even belong, become a pastor, or encourage others to join, welcoming them with open arms should they freely choose to do so.

If you are wondering about any or all of that, the only answer I can give you is this: This experience I have had and am still having of church . . . when push comes to shove, it all comes down to this: It is a love-hate relationship . . . That is what it is!! *It's about loving the church's ideals and despising the obstacles that get in the way of putting those ideals into practice.* More specifics will be found in the pages that lie ahead.

1

Hating What I Love

I ALWAYS FOUND IT FASCINATING how people develop the interests that we do. I was fortunate to have a lot of personal exposure to the variables in this process as for forty-three years of my life, I worked as either a teacher or counselor in schools, primarily on the high school level, with one eleven-year foray into the world of counseling young people in a middle school. This bivocational experience of having a full-time job in addition to my work as a church pastor turned out to be a wonderful resource for my ministry as a pastor, something about which I have written quite extensively over the years[1].

What always intrigued me about working with young people, especially in the thirty years I spent time as a school counselor, was finding out the *how* and the *why* behind their career interests and decisions. For some, quite honestly, it was the sense that they should live up to their parents' expectations. For others, it was the parents' insistence upon careers that drove them in the direction of something different. In reflecting on this, I could not help but do some self-examination, including considerable reflection upon the aspect of my life that was so connected to the institutional church and that, going many years back, had led me to consider ordained ministerial leadership within it.

In fact, the data gives evidence that for a growing number of people within our society, participation in the organized religious activities found

---

1. In my book *Part Time Pastor, Full Time Church (Pilgrim Press)* and in several of my published articles.

in houses of worship has been on the decline for several years. My experience with religion in both my formative years and in early adulthood has been quite different from what is reflected in those current trends. I had planned many years ago to be involved in religion on the institutional level, even to the point of flirting with and then eventually deciding to serve as a church leader in the role of a pastor, something I have done over the last twenty years. Even prior to that, I held positions within the organized institutional church as a teacher of religion, a director of religious education on the local church level and the broader institutional level of a Catholic diocese including my work as a youth ministry coordinator and eventually as an ordained permanent deacon within the church in which I was raised and eventually left at the age of 46.

So, what I am saying is that much of my life has been spent working in the field of institutional religion. I have been connected to church institutional structures such as dioceses and religious schools, youth ministry programs, synods, and conferences for most of my adult life. I have offered educational programs for both adolescents and adults in many different settings, both Catholic and Protestant. Heck, as a kid growing up, from the age of 8, much of my early morning time was spent serving Mass for nuns in a convent! In a time when many people of my age and a plethora of those who are younger have repudiated the practice of organized religion and have difficulty seeing its relevance, it has remained an integral part of my own life. Except for a few restless months in my late 30's when, technically, I was not affiliated with any particular religious denomination as well as a short period in the 1970's when I was sporadic with my church attendance, I have been connected to official organized religion for most of my life! Rare have been the periods of time when Sunday worship and church involvement were not an integral part of my regular routine! [2]

As I see it, it is interesting to enter into some self-reflection and wonder how I got to the place that I am, a place where I can say with certainty that my life and the life of organized Christianity have been bound together quite closely. However, and I think this is really important, while I cannot deny the importance of institutional religion in my life considering the fact that I have been ordained in two different church bodies, one Protestant, the other Roman Catholic, and have served as a pastor in two different

---

2. An interesting side note here is that the experience of staying away from church worship at very limited periods of my life gave me some helpful insights regarding why people make decisions not to go to church. In my conversations with these folks, I have found myself to be quite understanding regarding their perspective.

Hating What I Love

Protestant denominations and have worked in many Catholic parishes, as well as other institutions within the church, at the same time that I would have to state that there is much about this institution called church that I *love*, I also have to admit that there is much about it that bothers and annoys me as well, even to the point of stirring up within me some rather strong feelings of *hate*.

Now, before I go any further, I need to spend some time here defining and explaining the term hate as used within the context of that of which I am writing:

Here are some dictionary definitions of the word hate[3] *:*

1. *To feel extreme enmity toward*
2. *To have a strong aversion to . . .*

Of course, in this usage, it is important to spell out what the word enmity might mean as defined in that same dictionary:

The feeling of being actively opposed or hostile to someone or something.[4]

I have always tried to distinguish between having passionate feelings about issues, political positions or, in this case, policies and procedures found in churches and my attitude toward the people who hold them. In my view, any person who might happen to hold an opinion on a religious or political topic with which I strongly disagree, despise or, yes, hate, is a human being and daughter or son of God, someone who, simply put, *should not be hated and who must be treated with the respect due a child of God.* This distinction is extremely important and is clearly part of the message of Jesus, the driving force, I believe, beneath the Biblical injunction to love your enemies[5].Given the political climate in the United States at the time I am writing this, it is very easy to misunderstand this interpretation, an interpretation to which many have very little exposure as a result of the vitriolic language inherent in much of the language found primarily on the political right, as well as in certain religious circles!

Now, as I considered how I wanted to write this book, I found myself looking back at the experiences of my life with an eye toward the question of how I got so involved in institutional religion in the first place. That question, of course, quite naturally leads to an even deeper question: *What, for*

---

3. From the Merriam Webster Dictionary
4. See Merriam Webster Dictionary
5. Matthew 5:44

me, was and is the appeal of religion, more specifically faith, in the way that I seek to organize, structure and live my life?

I want to make something clear: There are an awful lot of people whom I know, people with whom I have worked and students whom I have taught, who might say they are *not really into religion* yet are individuals whom I would see as living examples of that which is good and true. These people are genuinely kind and giving to others, are repulsed at discriminatory behavior and are open to the goodness expressed by people of varied backgrounds and perspectives. For several reasons, they see what we might call organized religion as, at best, irrelevant and, at worse, quite harmful. Though my perspective is different from theirs, I often find myself quite sympathetic to their position. There are many times when I have cringed at the declarations of public figures and of preachers who, in my view, are distorting the message of Jesus. Unfortunately, I have known a good number of people who, while perceived by others to be religious, possess attitudes and tendencies that are exclusivist and, sad to say, even racist!

Yet, despite the reality of its flaws, I cannot deny that the church, as in organized Christianity, has been a significant and important part of my life. And with the understanding that my experience of it really has been what I would call *a love- hate relationship*, I think it is important that I explain a bit of how I got to a place wherein I could honestly reach that conclusion.

SO . . . LET'S BEGIN . . .

Through no choice of my own, when I was six years old, my parents enrolled me in the local, now nonexistent Catholic school in the small mill town in which I grew up[6]. It was the school my mother had attended several decades before. It was also a place in which the teaching was done by an order of religious sisters, popularly known, of course, as nuns, women with whom my mother was most familiar. My mom had a very close relationship with this order of sisters, the Daughters of the Holy Spirit, including having two cousins who were members of this order, and my sense as I look back at this time is that she was both really excited about the fact that I would be embarking upon a Catholic education and was quite certain that immersion in the practices and teachings of the Roman Catholic Church was the best possible way for me to live out my life. As was not unusual among

---

6. Putnam, Connecticut

Catholic mothers at the time, I also think her deep-seated hope was that I would one day become a priest!

The view of Catholicism in which I was raised was a fairly standard one back in the late 1950's and early into the next decade. Those baptized and raised in the Catholic tradition were expected to attend Mass regularly, faithfully observe holy days of obligation, practice fasting and abstinence during Lent, participate in a variety of seasonal Catholic rituals and, at a fairly young age, begin the practice of making a frequent confession.

As I grew up in a small mill town which was primarily populated by Catholics, my perception of the church was of the one that had the word Catholic in its title. This was reinforced through the teachings we received in school. In addition, in my little town, the *other churches* were so much smaller than the Catholic one my family attended[7], a church which offered the religious ritual known as *Mass* once a day during the week and three or four times come each Sunday morning. As a result, I learned very little about Protestantism in my Catholic elementary school experience. While I never experienced virulent attacks on the faith of Protestants whom I knew, the Catholic milieu in which I was raised sent out significant signals to us Catholic youth that we were being raised in what was commonly known to us Catholics as the one, true church.

In my second-grade year, which was really my first year in Catholic school as the principal suggested prior to the end of my first month there that I be advanced from first to second grade, a position for which I never would have advocated throughout my years working in the field of education, I prepared for and made my First Communion. However, according to the Catholic doctrine I was taught, one's soul had to be in the proper state to receive Communion worthily. To insure one's soul would be in so good a place, the Catholic had to learn about the sacramental experience of confession and the forgiveness of sin. Consequently, the day before my First Communion, I confessed my sins, i.e., whatever evil I may have committed as a six-year-old child, to a priest in the unique private space known as a confessional. This first-time practice would become for me a common one as from that time through at least my sophomore year in high school, it would be a practice of mine to go into my local church, usually on a Saturday evening, and confess my sins at least once a month, often twice. Looking back now, I cannot honestly remember what caused me at the time to break away from what had been a regular, virtually robotic practice,

---

7. St. Mary's Church, Putnam, Connecticut

the practice of consistent and very frequent confession. Maybe it was because Saturday night confession now interfered with the many high school dances my friends and I would attend either at my Catholic prep school or at one of the many all-female Catholic schools to which guys from our all-male school would travel on at least a couple of bus rides per month! More appealing than confession, I suppose!

Now, in fourth grade, something happened that had a significant impact upon my religious experience going forward, an impact that I speak of nostalgically up to this day. At the age of 8, I was afforded the opportunity and the responsibility to serve as an altar boy at the national Provincial House of the group of sisters (nuns) who taught me in my Catholic school and with whom my mom had so close a relationship and even happened to have a cousin who was a member of that community of nuns. In fact, it was quite common during the summers in my youth that one or more of these sisters would come to our home for a visit and often stay with us for several days! All of these experiences helped shape my comfort level with being around nuns. For many Catholics, in recounting their experience with sisters, there is a certain amount of fear attached. This is understandable as nuns in habits could be an imposing presence in the lives of children in Catholic schools. However, my experience was most definitively different.

As part of common practice in the Catholic Church, it was expected that the sisters would attend daily Mass, as well as Sunday worship, and that, as part of their experience, they would participate in a wide variety of ritual ceremonies that were part of Catholic life. These included ceremonies of religious profession as *women entered the convent life* and traditional Catholic rituals such as the Corpus Christi procession, the May crowning of Mary and many more. As a result, between my attendance at Catholic school and all the special events at which I assisted as part of this experience with the nuns, including many funerals of those beloved sisters who were members of that community, I had a very deep immersion in Roman Catholic life, including the role these many religious ceremonies played within it. It also did not hurt that when I was called upon to serve a sister's funeral, I was allowed to skip class at St. Mary's School for a good chunk of the day!

What I think is important here as I complete this book sixty years later, at the age of 69, is this:

At a very young age, without being able to identify my experience in these words, I was developing a deep love of the church. Though I could not articulate it then in words such as those I use today, as I reflect back upon those days and my own growth and development, these four things stand out:

1. In these experiences, without being able to really verbalize it, I found myself acquiring a *sense of the spiritual*. I found my world to be shaped by the belief that there was a spiritual reality in life far greater than I. Some theologians might describe this as an experience of *depth*[8].

2. That within these communities grounded in my Catholic religion, such as, the school I attended, the sisters who taught me there and those I knew from my altar boy life at what was affectionately called the nuns' Mother House, I found people who had a profound impact upon my own growing sense of spirituality within my life. I really liked most of those sisters with whom I came in contact over the years, women of different ages and perspectives, each of whom had a deep sense of really wanting to do something worthwhile with their "one, precious life."[9]

3. My first exposure to playing the piano and organ came from the opportunity to be taught by a nun who was a music teacher at my school. One day, as my grandmother was dying, this wonderful sister arranged for her to hear me play the organ over the telephone from the convent where I was receiving my lesson. As time went on and even while growing older, I remained connected to the people who resided at the Provincial House. I found myself rather close in age to those young women who were entering the convent and taking their first steps in religious life. In my later high school years, I would even share with them some of the literature I was reading in school, literature that tended not to find its way past the convent's front door! However, during this period of the late 1960's, major changes in professed religious life were beginning to take place. These included major changes in the clothing the sisters wore, which was more reflective of typical secular dress. This would be even more evident to me years later as I studied in graduate school with many women who were professed nuns.

4. The result of all of this is that I found myself quite comfortable in and deeply grounded by the religious communities of which I was a part at a very young age- my Catholic school, my local parish which sponsored the school and the sisters at the Mother House that had become

---

8. The distinguished theologian John Haught has done extensive writing in this area.
9. A phrase inspired by the poet Mary Oliver.

over the years the center of my religious practice, populated by some great, committed women and the wonderful priest [10] who served them.

Whenever I have found myself taking a retroactive look, I have always caught myself concluding that it was because of these experiences that I became deeply grounded and rooted in my faith and I saw the *spiritual experience* as an integral part of my life. I have reflected on this as I have thought back to how wonderful it was to have had the opportunity to get to know those nuns who taught me as I assisted at Mass from my years as a little boy right up to the time when I graduated from high school.

I recall nostalgically and gratefully the years I spent at the Provincial House and all of the wonderful sisters I met there as well as some of my former teachers at my Catholic school, St. Mary's in Putnam, Connecticut, which, quite sadly, just closed a few years back, a clear-cut example of much of the anguish institutional Catholicism has endured. I recall with great fondness traveling with my parents to visit my second-grade teacher when she was transferred to oversee a group of sisters in Massachusetts. I remember a summer trip with my parents up to a town on the Canadian border and visiting some nuns there, one who was a cousin of my mom. Even to this day, sixty years since I first stepped into that mother house to learn how to serve the then Latin Roman Catholic Mass, whenever I return to my hometown, I take a ride by that imposing facility which housed these wonderful women, a special space containing within it " the altar of God, the God who gave joy to my youth."[11]

Though the Provincial House in my home town which housed so many nuns over the years is now a building converted into a *for profit* secular private school, there remains something rather special for me whenever I enter its gates and pause to remember my days on its grounds! *My experience of all those years there, quite frankly, have had a lifelong impact upon my spirituality.* When I visit my parents' graves at the Catholic cemetery in my hometown of Putnam, I so often stop by the graves of so many of those beloved sisters, their collective resting places calling to mind for me the impact they had and always will have upon my life. As time has moved along,

---

10. The late Rev. Yves Guenver who served as Chaplain to the sisters at their Provincial House.

11. These words are taken from the pre-Vatican II Mass and are translated from the original Latin.in my early altar boy days I and my fellow servers at Mass would say the varied responses at Mass in Latin. Many of those prayer responses remain with me to this day.

Hating What I Love

I often pause with amazement at how they touched my life so powerfully, even as I know that within the institutional system of the church of that day, women, including these sisters, were treated as second class citizens, unlike those men who were ordained to the ministry of Catholic priest.

As I look backward, even though as I write this, I am a former Catholic, having left the church of my youth twenty-three years prior to writing this book, I find myself deeply grateful for the visceral sense of spirituality I found through these experiences. As a result of them, I discovered that I had a deep interest in what we call *religion*. I evolved in my interest of what religion taught, of the varieties of religious experiences, of the pluralism in religious practices, and of the expectations of those who served in leadership roles. I also found myself interested in those incredible people throughout the course of history who stood up for Christian values and principles, often quite heroically.

This young boy found himself intrigued and excited about seeing movies about the miracles at Fatima, and about heroic figures such as Thomas Becket, Francis of Assisi and Thomas More. The sisters at my Catholic school oftentimes accompanied entire classes to some of these screenings! I liked going to Mass. I really liked the many nuns I knew. I enjoyed talking to priests. I was fascinated by what led them to make the decision to enter the priesthood, even more so when I began to understand what celibacy entailed. My participation in the Catholic experience was one of the most important touch points in my life, right up there with my concurrent, passionate love of baseball and all the heroes present in my obsession with the Boston Red Sox.

With this grounding I have described, I discovered how interested I was in learning more about bold and heroic fellow Christians throughout the course of history. Over time, this included members and heroes of the Catholic Church, for sure, but also found itself broadening out to take in other individuals I had come to see as role models for how to live out one's Christian faith, which I somehow had come to perceive as deeply integral to my existence.

I continued to develop in my interest and participation in Catholicism. Through the influence of a wonderful young priest at the Catholic prep school I attended, I enjoyed learning about thinkers such as Thomas Aquinas and Pierre Teilhard de Chardin, discovering along the way that faith and reason were not incompatible. This recognition took me a step beyond what I had internalized through the process of learning and reciting answers from the traditional catechism[12]. In fact, I discovered that faith and reason really needed to go hand in hand with one another.

Over time, my influences started to shift a bit as I grew to discover heroic voices both within and outside of the Catholic Church. These included inspirational thinkers and activists such as Jean Paul Sartre, Albert Camus, Rev. Dr. Martin Luther King (a Protestant pastor!), Cesar Chavez, Daniel and Philip Berrigan, Dorothy Day and many more.

It was in my early high school years, however, that I became consciously aware of some changes that were taking place within me. Of course, I was entering adolescence, a seismic change in and of itself, and while that affected some of my interests, for sure, I also found myself asking an awful lot of questions and challenging myself to think more thoroughly about some of life's important issues.

It was in my sophomore year of high school, when while on the road to a Red Sox doubleheader in Boston, that I saw a book in the mall's bookstore which intrigued me with its title, *A Modern Priest Looks at His Outdated Church*[13]. I persuaded my parents to buy it for me. I was mesmerized by what I read within it from the moment I started reading it in the back seat on the road to Fenway Park that afternoon. As a result, I found myself questioning many of the positions that were part and parcel of my lifelong Catholic faith. I discovered a high level of discomfort with many rules and regulations of my church. For the very first time in my life, *I found myself having some powerful gut level visceral feelings which suggested to me that this church that I had loved and that was so special to me throughout my life also had some rather deep and profound flaws.*

I began to question where the church stood on a wide variety of issues. My emerging sense of questioning happened to coincide with the dissent ridden response to Pope Paul VI's encyclical on birth control, *Humanae Vitae*[14]. Increasingly aware of the fact that I had given thought to the Catholic priesthood as a career choice and experiencing the developing stage of adolescence, I was certainly drawn to James Kavanaugh's insights as he questioned mandatory celibacy for priests. Though in 1968, the movement in favor of ordaining women to the Catholic priesthood was in its nascent stage, the impetus to do so struck me as making a lot of sense. In addition,

12. *The Baltimore Catechism*
13. James Kavanaugh, Simon and Schuster, 1967
14. Issued in 1968. This encyclical affirmed the position that the use of artificial birth control was unacceptable for Catholics.

the church's teaching on several questions of sexuality, as well as its approach to divorce and remarriage, struck me as needing a good deal of rethinking.

This was also a period in which I was increasingly aware of the presence of significant dissent within the Roman Catholic Church, the church of my youth. While this dissent may have been bubbling up for years under the surface, at this time it became a quite noticeable presence! It manifested itself in the calls for reform in the areas I just mentioned. In addition, it was during this period that Catholics began to see evidence of some movement away from the practice of mandatory Mass attendance. In fact, the ways in which many Catholics understood *sin* was undergoing an awful lot of change. Some behaviors which had been considered objectively sinful in Catholic moral teaching were now challenged by highly respected Catholic theologians. Requirements about weekly Mass attendance and reception of Communion began to be interpreted more loosely. To paraphrase my favorite musician, *"the times were indeed a changing"*[15] and this was happening in the Roman Catholic Church, the church of my youth and my neighborhood!

I also noticed that during this time the Catholic priesthood as well as the convent life of many Catholic women were undergoing significant changes. Dedicated men and women were opting to find ways to serve God other than within the traditional confines of these vocations. The theology of the church was evolving to consider the varied ways in which one engages in ministry and the word ministry itself had been expanded to define lives of service lived by those not ordained or committed to the vows taken by those in religious orders of women or men. The concept of *lay ministry engaged in by those who were not ordained* began taking on some significant momentum. There was a massive proliferation of opportunities for lay people to earn graduate degrees and to serve in parishes and on college and high school campuses in professional positions in religious education and pastoral ministry once limited to priests, brothers [16] and nuns.

As I moved into college life at a college run by the Jesuits, formally and officially known as the Society of Jesus, the combination of wonderful professors and priests on campus as well as my own developing and

---

15. This phrase is inspired by the words of Bob Dylan's song.

16. A brother was a man who was not an ordained priest but who, similar to sisters, took vows of poverty, chastity and obedience and lived within a religious community of others who did the same.

emerging questions made for an amazing period of religious tension and growth. I truly loved the spiritual atmosphere of the college I attended. Yet, I was also fully aware of the fact that the campus on which I resided was far different from what it had been years and decades prior. On the day I entered, the President lifted restrictions on visitations in the dorms and soon thereafter, plans were put in place for this all-male institution to go fully coeducational by my junior year. Daily Mass attendance, long a requirement on this campus, was no longer part of this college's life. Fortunately, in my opinion, virtually all of the most highly renowned Catholic colleges made the decision to admit women and today a single sex Catholic college is quite rare. At the time, it was considered a radical move by many within the church and/or among its alumni/ae and met with some significant resistance! Some children of my college's alumni who were students when I was were quite vehement in their opposition. On the flip side, others were very happy about the decision. It was not unusual to see intense debates on the topic take place within the school's dorms. Personally, I was thrilled!

This was a period of rapid change and dissent within Catholicism and American society as well. There were major turns in the direction of putting faith into practice. It was a period when the Catholic peace movement was alive and active, reflected in my school's relationship with the Berrigan brothers, Catholic priests who were peace activists and stood in powerful opposition to the Vietnam War, including their participation in significant acts of civil disobedience. On ABC TV news one night, Howard K. Smith referred to my college as *"the cradle of the New Catholic Left"*. I took that as a definite compliment to my school!

During this period, I detected some significant shifts in what was going on within me spiritually. I was fascinated by the reading I was doing in my theology classes and was drawn to learning more about Christianity as understood outside of the Roman Catholic context. I visited many Protestant churches both in Worcester and when I returned to my hometown for breaks from school. In many of those visits, I would try to make a connection with the church's pastor and participate in their educational forums. In many cases, I would arrange for meetings with the church's clergy at some point later that week. At the same time, I found peace and serenity simply by stepping into the beautiful chapel on my college campus, replete with all the feel of traditional Catholicism around me, providing a safe space for me even as I questioned some of the beliefs on display in this sacred place. I would begin every Lenten morning in one of my collegiate years by stopping by the chapel, oftentimes spending time there alone, many times with the "liturgy of the hours"[17] in my hand, a great place to go as I began my day.

When I entered Holy Cross, I was expecting to major in Political Science and/or English and perhaps to do a double major. My initial career goal was to be a lawyer for labor unions and eventually to move into the world of politics. However, I was most fortunate in that during my first year, I had some wonderful professors in the areas of philosophy and theology. I found the readings and study in those fields to be fascinating!

For some reason, one day when I walked into the school's administration building, a bulletin board posting caught my eye. It was a request for students to volunteer to teach religious education to junior high school students at a Catholic parish in a suburb a few miles away from the college. I thought it would be wonderful to share some of my newly discovered insights with young people who were part of a changing Catholic church!

When I looked into this further, I had a basic concern. The parish was a few miles away and I did not have access to a car. I soon discovered that the person responsible for coordinating this program was the church's Director of Religious Education, a Roman Catholic nun. This woman told me and the others who called offering to volunteer that she would provide us with a weekly ride to classes. As it turned out, two things happened because of my decision to volunteer to teach CCD. First, I enjoyed the many conversations in the car each week with the wonderful sister who coordinated this program. She was bright, inquisitive and a great example of someone trying to present Christianity to young people in a positive, even exciting and relevant light! Secondly, I learned that I really liked both thinking about and teaching theology. This discovery would eventually shape my shift in academic major[18]. I had entered college expecting to go on to law school after graduation. As a result of many experiences first shaped by this one, I graduated with my career focus radically changed!

---

17. Also known as the Breviary, this book included prayers to be said at various times during the day. These prayers were required for Catholic clergy as well as for religious sisters. Those in monasteries were expected to gather for prayer even more frequently than others obliged to do these prayers. After the Second Vatican Council, this mode of praying was widely opened to the non-ordained or professed within the Catholic Church.

18. I had originally declared as a Political Science major and then shifted to English. Along the way, I also took some courses in Religious Studies, which would become my eventual major.

In addition, I also really liked and appreciated the alternative worship experiences that became part of my college life. This included daily celebrations of the Eucharist (Mass) in the more informal downstairs chapel. It was there that I experienced a worship that felt so much more personal than that of the traditional worship upon which I was raised. There was a beautiful simplicity in the ways that we gathered, heard the Word, discussed it and shared a meal that actually conveyed the sense of being a meal, all preparing us to be sent out to live our college lives and ultimately our post-graduation ones as well, both inspired and nurtured by the experiences we would share in our time in that chapel. In addition, I had wonderful experiences of Sunday evening Mass in the residential suite of the Jesuit priest who lived on my floor in Alumni Hall.

I have a funny side story to tell in this regard! Many, many years later, in my late 60's, as I was serving as a pastor in a Protestant church, a woman came up to me at the end of the service who was very, very concerned! She had seen that on that morning, when it got to the part of the service when we called to mind the Last Supper, I had not stood behind the altar where the pastor would usually stand. Instead, I had set up a little table in front of the altar and *sat down* through the words of institution of this Eucharistic celebration.

This truly wonderful, faithful, and kind woman asked me if I was feeling OK. Honestly, I had no idea why she was asking me that. So, I inquired of her! What she then told me was that she noticed that I had sat down when I called to mind Jesus' words from the Last Supper and suspected that maybe I was feeling sick. The reality is that the influence from those celebrations of Communion in my college days have *always* had a profound impact upon my life and the fact remains that, *given the choice between a vertical and horizontal approach to worship, I would inevitably choose the horizontal.* I told her that if I ever had had the opportunity to design a church, the table (altar} would be amid the people with all of us gathered around it!

Somewhere along the line, most likely influenced by the daily Masses at Holy Cross, I became quite conscious of the differences between a *horizontal* and a *vertical* approach to worship. It struck me as unusual that everything in churches and chapels was located *up there* where those in charge of presiding at worship were stationed. When I experienced the horizontal approach downstairs in my college chapel, my eyes were opened, and I started thinking in terms of what the institutional church had done to make the shift between the original intent of worship and what become established liturgical custom. In fact, this vertical approach remained even within most Protestant practice, although at Protestantism's core was the reality of *reform!*

As I write this, I am certain that any liturgical traditionalists reading this book are currently cringing! You see, it had become rather clear to me that when Jesus ate the Last Supper, He did so while surrounded by his closest friends around a table. I had learned also that it was customary for early Christians to celebrate Communion within the context of a meal within a home. I also discovered that during this time that many Catholic priests, including married ones, were celebrating what would come to be known as home Masses on Sunday mornings, providing alternatives for many who were turned off by the worship style in their local parishes. As a matter of fact, one of the most beautiful Sunday worship gatherings I have ever experienced was at the at home celebration of the First Communion of the child of one of my college professors, which included Communion bread that was homemade and inspired by the Scriptural passage regarding the peaceable kingdom[19]. The priest presiding at this was someone whose Saturday evening liturgies I came to experience as I would often travel from Worcester to Boston for a Saturday evening worship at Boston University at which he presided!

These college experiences of worship, coupled with what I began reading back in my high school days, helped to move me in the direction of embracing a Jesus centric approach to my faith. It also did not hurt that I took a phenomenal course simply entitled *Jesus*, taught by the Jesuit college chaplain I admired so much[20]! Raised in a Catholic tradition that emphasized specific doctrines and teachings as essential, I then began focusing more on the fact that what Jesus suggested and implied in his life were truly the essentials for the ways we constructed our lives. While respecting the Catholic theological heritage and the importance of the use of the mind in terms of developing one's religious affirmations, I also embraced the approach to individual conscience which I found reflected in the writings of Protestant reformers, so powerfully inspired by Martin Luther. Without being able to verbalize it at the time, I realize in retrospect that Luther's approach known as *adiaphora*[21] was a really good way to approach many issues in institutional

---

19. Isaiah 11:1–9
20. The late Rev. Robert Manning, S. J.
21. Some even claim that, at core, a good definition of this might be 'whatever'.

religion. Simply put, this concept allows for a corrective to legalism in its recognition of the importance of distinguishing the essential in worship from that which is nonessential, opening the door for offering liturgical worship which can respond to the needs and context of its participants as well as provide for new ways of celebration to those who have become used to doing liturgy the same way repeatedly.

Not certain of which direction I would pursue for a career, I entered my post collegiate experience without a real sense of a long-term plan. I gave serious thought to entering a Catholic seminary and becoming a priest. I arranged for meetings with priests and those responsible for coordinating applications for the priesthood in several dioceses. Had I opted for the priesthood, my ministry would have drawn on the inspiration of those leaders within the Catholic Church who pushed the envelope and challenged the institutional church on many of its practices. Ultimately, I concluded that there were many ways to be of service that did not entail embracing mandatory celibacy. To be clear, I respect the commitment to celibacy taken by many individuals. However, I do not see where that is a necessary requirement for a woman or a man in terms of being a faithful and effective ordained leader, a leader Roman Catholics call a priest.

If you opt to read my book *Crossing the Street*, you can read in complete detail about my eventual transition into Protestant Christianity. This transition needs to be understood in terms of what continues to be *very real* for me even in my eventual shift to being ordained and serving churches in the Protestant tradition which I have been doing since the year 2001.

As you will notice a few times as you travel your way through this book, I have what I would call **a love-hate relationship** *with the organized, institutional church.* This became rather obvious throughout my Catholic years and though Protestantism *is* a place where I feel very comfortable, despite that comfort, this love/hate relationship with institutional religion is still very much alive- and Protestant practices are not exempt!! Nonetheless, below you will find how I would have described it back in my Catholic days as well as what I think about the tradition of Protestantism, which many years ago, I embraced as my own.

Technically, it refers to certain doctrines or practices which are indifferent because they are neither commanded nor forbidden in Scripture.

Hating What I Love

WHAT BOTHERS ME ABOUT THE CHURCH IN WHICH I WAS RAISED:

(Translation: Things I really hate in no particular order)

- The teaching on birth control
- The insistence on annulments as a requirement for remarriage and policies on divorce and remarriage, including reception of Communion
- The lack of recognition of separation of church and state as expressed in many political positions, most passionately the issue of abortion
- The tendency to seek to impose one's practices on others in a religiously pluralistic nation
- The insistence on required personal confession as well as the rules surrounding it
- Some issues with Eucharistic theology
- A heavy insistence on intractable doctrine
- The preponderance of habit and routine in religious practice.
- The overall understanding of sexuality
- The concept and practice of indulgences
- A position on intercession of the deceased that strikes me as somewhat extreme
- The denial of ordination to women
- A hesitancy toward singing
- The concept and practice of annulments

THOSE THINGS I DEEPLY APPRECIATE IN THE CHURCH IN WHICH I WAS RAISED

- Incredible Catholic role models e.g., Dorothy Day, Pope Francis, Oscar Romero, Daniel Berrigan, Francis of Assisi . . . and many more . . .
- Outstanding theologians and writers- Aquinas, Augustine, Karl Rahner, Teilhard de Chardin, Hans Kung, Richard McBrien, Avery

Dulles, Richard Rohr, Ilia Delio, John Haught, Elizabeth Johnson and more...

- A variety of means of prayer and the monastic tradition. I have had great experiences visiting places such as the St. Joseph's Abbey of Trappist monks in Massachusetts and Weston Priory in Vermont. These are very special places for prayer and are now frequented by many Protestants as well as Roman Catholics.
- The liturgy of the hours as a way of structuring one's prayer life and connecting to a broader world, a liturgy that has inspired liturgy in Protestant church traditions, including among Anglicans and Lutherans
- The variety of religious communities e.g. Franciscans, Sisters of Mercy, Paulists, Dominicans, Jesuits and the uniqueness of each, all providing special gifts to the broader church
- A broad, expansive, and developed Eucharistic theology
- A visible model of church unity as found in the Bishop of Rome. Note: This does not mean that I hold to the understanding of the Papacy as understood within Roman Catholicism. It does affirm the important role of a bishop who serves a unifying function within the wider church community.

THINGS I APPRECIATE DEEPLY IN THE CHURCH TRADITION I HAVE FREELY CHOSEN:

- The potential for diversity of practice
- The built-in capacity for acceptance of different approaches
- Means to offer unity rather than division
- Acceptance of the strengths of other religious traditions
- A desire to stay away from legalism
- Great theologians- Bonhoeffer, Luther, Tillich, Niebuhr and many more... This includes excellent Biblical scholarship as well...

THOSE THINGS THAT BOTHER ME IN THE CHURCH TRADITION I HAVE FREELY CHOSEN:

- The ways in which churches have split off from one another. This includes the fact that there are several types of churches that might call themselves by the same name, e.g., Lutheran, but in many ways remain radically separate from one another. I find it hard to explain to folks why, for example, the Lutheran Church of which they are a part is not necessarily on the same page as other Lutherans or why. It is difficult to explain all the breakaway branches in that church. Another example is that Congregationalists may be found both in and out of the United Church of Christ! In my mind, all of this is reflective of an unfortunate division within the community of the church of Jesus Christ! Very sad . . .
- A lack of appreciation for the roots of their traditions and theology. Simply put: Many Protestant churches do not teach members about the Catholic- Protestant points of connection.
- Misunderstandings of other Protestant denominations, as well as Roman Catholicism.
- Deficits in education offered for members/friends of all ages. For a variety of reasons, slippages in this area have become more apparent in recent years.

The Protestant tradition is strongly divided between those who advocate for a literal reading of Scripture and those who seek to emphasize the means in which those books selected to be included in the Bible were selected. Mainline Protestants are comfortable with the fact that not all Biblical passages need be taken literally. Likewise, some very conservative Protestant communities hold opinions which contradict science and its value.

AND SO . . .

The title of this chapter is *Hating What I Love*. While hate is something to avoid when dealing with and describing our relationship with others, it is totally legitimate to talk in terms of despising certain practices and traditions that have accrued within the world of religion over the years. If one is to claim that she/he hates or despises the fact that the church of which she/

I Love the Church, I Hate the Church

he is a member seems not to put an emphasis on ongoing religious education and if one to say that he/she hatred that fact, that declaration of hate is, in fact, an affirmation of love.

In what you just read, I identify some things that I find myself despising or *hating* in the church tradition of my youth. One thing I mention as being hate worthy is the position of that church on making homosexuals feel uncomfortable about their sexual orientation. The passion one might engender in taking a position that declares a hatred for the position espoused by, in this case, a church, presumes this: *It presumes that this hatred is centered on the fact that one hates or despises a position taken because it does not provide the sense of love for the other that Christian faith entails.* One could therefore despise the fact that one is excluded for Communion out of love for the person and the belief that one could find spiritual benefit by sharing in Communion. *One would therefore be applying the values of her/his faith by hating not the person who applies the rule but the rule itself. This is a crucial distinction!*

Consequently, as I reflect upon my relationship with the institutional church, the relationship I have experienced throughout my life, I find myself experiencing the reality of a love-hate relationship. *I find it quite honest to say that, at one and the same time, I can both love and hate the church! It is easy to find myself despising those impediments that stand in the way of what the church is expected to be. I hate that fact and it is ok to say that. In fact, the very reason I hate it is because of the love I have for what the church, in ideal form, is really intended to be.*

I hope that makes sense to you. In addition, I hope you give it some serious thought and engage in discussions with others about your feelings toward it! I also hope you find a way to talk to others about how they might perceive this reality of hating what they love as they might experience it within

the organized, institutional church! Through the rest of this book, I hope to point out some tendencies, practices, and traditions that one could readily as describe as *hate worthy*, traditions that get in the way of the church's great potential for shaping both individual lives and those of the broader world!

2

WHERE THERE IS HATRED, LOVE

Where there is hatred, let me sow love

—PRAYER OF FRANCIS OF ASSISI

I AM GOING TO BEGIN this chapter by describing a situation:

You have been invited by a friend of yours to visit her church. It is one that you have never set foot in prior to this invitation. On the morning of the church service, upon your entrance into the building, you are handed a flyer encouraging participation in the church's *latest fundraising campaign*. The promotional literature implies that donating x amount of money during this drive would be a great way to *serve Jesus!* The literature indicates that a wonderful way to spread the *love of Jesus* might be to provide the funds to expand the building and buy new audio-visual equipment to spice up the services so they could have a broader appeal and could even reach those at home not inclined to show up at a church! This campaign could also help in providing the necessary air conditioning for the inevitable hot and humid days in the church's geographic location and/or provide for heating the building should the church be faced with cold winters ahead.

As the worship service unfolded, the theme for the day centered on the promotion of this fundraising campaign with Scripture passages offered to the congregation which would drive home the message of *giving*. In fact, depending upon the preferences of its pastor and lay leadership, you may even get an exposure to the term *stewardship* as well! Lay church leaders might even get up to speak about how excited they are to be starting this new campaign. You most likely will hear them use that word *stewardship* with great excitement afloat in their voices! The music director also obviously worked closely with the pastor in a full-fledged attempt to integrate music with the powerful words of invitation to this important, groundbreaking and potentially growth inducing event in the church's life!

So, what do you think?

Let's get even more direct and practical:

If you are overwhelmed with excitement about this, what, if anything, is your reaction saying? Let me suggest that it could speak to your sense of *hope* for the church's future at a time when you know that churches are closing or turning to part time pastors because they cannot afford a full time one! You may be thinking *that this won't happen to your church!*

Let's say instead that you absolutely despise what you are experiencing at this church service because it seems as though this church is fixated on money. What if your mind starts wandering and you think about people who really enjoy your church but realistically cannot be expected to dig deep and turn over hundreds of dollars they need to spend on rent or a mortgage or maybe food or child support for their kids? *Is it possible that lying beneath your discomfort and actual hatred for this experience is found a tremendous sense of idealism and a deeply rooted love for the church, the church the way that it is really intended to be, a church that, in its very beginnings, set out to meet the needs of those who were impoverished and needed support?*[1]

As you know from the information I offered about my background in the last chapter, the institution known as church has been an important part of my life. If push were to come to shove and someone were to ask me what I felt about the church and were to push me a little further and ask whether I would say that I loved it, my answer would be that I do. Yet, having given that answer, I would also tell the person that I would like the opportunity to explain myself even further and to be as clear as I can.

Why would I even suggest this? Isn't it enough to say that one really *does* love the church? Yet, you see, it is nowhere near being that simple. In fact, if asked to explain, I would follow up by saying that *there is an awful lot about the church that I hate as well.* Now, for an ordained clergyperson to even suggest or imply that he/she might in any way *have the word hate*

---

1. Please take a close look at the book of Acts of the Apostles in the New Testament.

associated with her/his opinions about the church would sound threatening to some, maybe even teetering on the edge of heretical. Having said that, it needs to be clear that the word heresy refers to beliefs or church doctrine. *It is not intended to describe differences of opinion regarding such practical church matters as a building drive or providing for climate controls in one's worship space!*

I can just hear the voices of many leaders (and followers) in the world of organized religion who would quarrel quite passionately about my conclusion. Some who are part of some church traditions or denominations might argue that this institution we call church was founded by Jesus Christ, the incarnate presence of God. Others would contend that this community of church is affirmed by the Bible. Still others would invoke Biblical and theological terminology and claim that when you are talking about the church, what you are describing is the *Body of Christ*, a descriptive phrase found in much of church literature. Some, I am sure, would argue quite passionately and vociferously that *hate is simply NOT a word one should use in describing what one thinks about the church!*

Yet, I am very sincere when I make the point *that I do have a love- hate relationship with the church.'* If challenged to explain what I mean, here is what I would say:

I love . . .

- *The fact that this entity called church is seen as a community. i.e., people who have something significant in common. When I hear or sing "Blest be the tie that binds[2]", I can feel this quite deeply and viscerally!*
- *The reality that what this community of church shares with one another is a commitment to the teachings, memory, and life of Jesus of Nazareth.*
- *The fact that there is a universality to this community and a connection with communities of faith throughout the world. While this church is part of a local community, it is likewise connected to the universal Body of Christ.*
- *That the church is tasked with keeping the memory of Jesus alive and proclaiming His presence within us and around us.*
- *The fact that the church is also charged specifically with taking the teachings of Jesus and putting them into practice in the real world.*

---

2. A traditional Christian hymn also used as a backdrop in some productions of Thornton Wilder's *Our Town*.

- *That the church has the responsibility and potential to offer hope, justice, and peace as ideals in the real world and to work on behalf of these lofty goals. The church has the potential to offer an honest, intelligent challenge to racism, sexism, homophobia, and violence. In short, the church has great potential to be a prophetic voice within a culture that has shown itself capable of going in the wrong direction in so many ways. In addition, it can serve as a prophetic voice within the broader church, which, quite sadly, is often not quite as prophetic as it should be.*

Yet, on the other hand, there are things about the church that I can also say I hate. Here are but a few:

I hate . . .

- That the church, allegedly built on the teachings of Jesus, has throughout history often been on the side of the privileged and the prejudiced. I think of the writings of Frederick Douglass and many other slaves who told tales of their segregated seating at the churches of their youth. I think of the words of Dr. King that *11 o'clock on Sunday morning is the most segregated hour of the entire week.*[3]

- That elements within the church, while on the one hand espousing the value of Christianity, readily justify attitudes and actions that clearly contradict the explicit teachings of the One they claim to follow. In other words, Jesus.

- That the institutional church, founded on the teachings and actions of one who declared God as the center of life, all too easily takes on the structure and the values of the culture within which it exists. Think of the structure of town or city governments and then consider the structure of leadership in the church. Pretty similar, wouldn't you say? Now, to be fair, some might argue that building a church leadership structure based on the models that evolved within the government of the United States is not necessarily a bad thing, right? After all, our nation is a democratic republic and electing leaders to represent the best interests of the people, in this case the people who constitute the body of the church, is really a good thing! However, as is the case with governmental leaders, those chosen to govern need to keep their ears to the ground and act in the interest of those whom they represent.

---

3. This was a well-known statement that Dr. King used quite often in sermons, speeches, and interviews.

We have seen many examples of how this has not always been put into practice, both in civil society and within the institution of the church. Without negating the importance of this in the world of politics, it is important to point out that the inspiration for church leadership is the servant leadership model lived by Jesus and espoused by those early believers who would be His disciples.

- That, over the course of history, church leaders have developed doctrines and dogmas which they claim as absolute, yet which proceed to raise certain troubling questions and challenges.
- That many a church institution responds to the challenges it faces by creating a climate wherein people feel uncomfortable within that church. Throughout church history, there have been many well-known examples of practices and policies centered on exclusion.

Quite honestly, these above statements contain information about the institutional church that upset me and cause me a good deal of disillusion, even what some would call an experience of *agita*[4] within. *The fact is that I have a lifelong relationship with this institution called church, an institution that has nurtured and nourished me and one that, quite honestly, I love very, very much!*

However, within this institution, there are things that:

- Make me angry
- Strike me as being antithetical to what the church is supposed to be all about

Consequently, I do find myself despising, yes, even *hating*, those conditions within church life which detract from the church's ideals. These ideals of which I write are based on the teachings, life, and example of the man Jesus of Nazareth. *In short, it **is** safe to say that I really do **hate** how so often the church focuses on things other than the core teachings of Jesus.*

In this chapter, I have already identified and described some of these pet peeves of mine. As you continue to read, you will find yourself reading about even more of them. Yet, to provide for you a listing and an explanation that makes any kind of sense, it is important that I lay out for you some of my core beliefs which should shed light upon the expectations I would

---

4. Discomfort

have of the institutional church. Let me begin in no order, though you may want to think through them and prioritize them yourselves:

- I expect that a church should be a place of *welcoming*. To me, that means that, in policy and attitude, the church is open to people of different sexual orientations and lifestyles, as well as a range of opinions. *I long for a church where people of left, right and center can respect one another and engage in healthy conversation and dialogue* surrounding important issues within the church, the nation, and the world.

- I also believe the church should be a safe place for both adults and children where people are accepted for who they are.

- Though I consider myself as opinionated and on the progressive end of the Christian spectrum, I also believe the church should be a place of healthy dialogue and diversity of specific opinions, as I note above. *I affirm the fact that much of faith is mystery and, consequently, those connected to church should be open to opportunities to explore varied interpretations of teachings and practices within the church community.*

- I expect that a church will find ways to get people interested in learning. I believe it is important to provide opportunities for people to engage in study of the Bible, church history and the variety of different approaches to religion operative in our world. As I see it, most members and friends of congregations have a background in formal religious education that may very well have stopped at the time they were confirmed. As they became adults and confronted the moral implications of adult decisions, their churches may very well not have provided for them the resources to reflect on moral decision making as an adult Christian! Ethics is quite complex. As a teacher of moral theology, I often emphasized this statement of mine to my students: *"What appears to be absolute in the abstract is often ambiguous in the concrete situation".*[5] Providing adolescents and adults with opportunities to think through the complexities of moral decision making should be an important task of the church!

- High on my list is the conviction that a church community sees itself as promoting harmony, understanding and empathy.

---

5. This is a statement I developed as I was preparing to teach a class in the area of moral theology.

- I expect a church to have a passion for the needs of people beyond its walls. I look for a church to see itself as *outward gazing*. This does not detract from the commitment a church must have to its members and friends, but it moves the local church beyond a comfortable club like entity toward a position where there is significant outward focus and awareness.
- I expect a church to be a place of *inquiry*. In this context, I would look for a church to provide opportunities for in depth learning on significant theological and moral issues.
- I expect that a church will offer meaningful worship (liturgy). This worship would be attentive to the core of Christian worship as expressed in a variety of forms. This church would find a robotic like sense of weekly worship unfulfilling. Meaningful worship includes variety in its approach to music. This entails blending traditional and contemporary sounds, as well as a multiplicity of available musical sources, both secular and sacred. It also means an openness to using the resources of a broad array of musical traditions. My experience of many Catholic and Protestant churches is that so often, in their selection of hymns, the tendency is to stick primarily with those hymns that have been part of their tradition. To be clear, Lutherans *should sing A Mighty Fortress is our God* [6], for example. Likewise, Catholics should sing *Holy God, We Praise Thy Name*[7]. In addition, I believe that churches should expect their pastors to have a good working knowledge of a broader range of liturgical music, both in terms of its trends and its theology.

    However, it is in the best interest of the broader Christian experience that Protestants and Catholics alike incorporate variety into their musical selections. Some may ask' Why?'? As I see it, there are many ways of describing one's faith and by offering a variety of hymn options representing different cultures, styles, and theologies, one broadens one's perspective regarding the Christian message, moving it out of the realm of provincialism into the wider arena of a universal approach to the mystery of God's presence and the centrality of Jesus' life in the one who calls oneself a follower of Christ!

---

6. The famous hymn written by Martin Luther

7. A well known and much beloved Roman Catholic hymn, sung often in my days serving Mass at the Provincial House!

Within the context of these expectations, I would share some of the behaviors and decisions I have seen in churches throughout my lifetime that I can say with honesty I have found quite easy to despise. I know that some people reading this would say that my expectations for the institutional church are too high. Yet, I would contend that it is important to have high expectations when one is dealing with an institution that exists for the sake of inspiring people with the message of Jesus! If the sermons are so bland and trite and blasé that they leave the listeners bored and sensing no connections between the spoken, preached words and their own lives, how remiss would that church be in terms of adequately and compellingly conveying the message of Jesus, who is the reason for the existence of that church in the first place. Likewise, the same would be true should its music be so dull and robotic that it fails the test of touching and stirring the worshiping soul and I would even add, sometimes going to places it never had expected to go!

Likewise, if local churches do not inspire individuals to invite others to experience their life or if they do not promote significant, reflective thinking about the connection between worship and living out the Christian life, then is it any surprise that people are not motivated to attend? I would also argue that if a church offers no concrete ways to reach out and help others in need and to have the consciousness of those who attend that church raised so that they may gain a deeper awareness of the reality of human needs, that church has a definite problem, the problem of not fully embracing the message of Jesus!

My contention here is that the emotion of hate when applied to the way churches may be structured or with respect to their approach to theology, liturgy and education speaks to a love for the potential for what a church should be. In fact, yes, where what drives the church is the Gospel message or the concept of a Christian community, the deep-down truth is that this so-called hatred for what this church has made of itself is really a sign of love for the potential of the church to be what it should be-a community attentive to the ideals made visible in the life of Jesus of Nazareth.

My point is that were one to investigate the history of significant changes within institutions, one would find that those promoting the change found themselves troubled by the way lofty ideals were so often not really implemented in practice. An institution(church), that exists because of a man of peace has so readily defended the practice of war throughout the course of history. It often has often been guilty of being complicit in its acceptance of wartime activity of questionable moral merit. A community born of the inclusive love of God as expressed in Jesus has all too often conveyed the message, often in subtle ways, *that only some, not all,* are welcome! Throughout the course of history and most noticeably over these last few years, many church communities have been all too willing to express support for politicians who in their view promote Christian values while at the same time have helped to create a climate of hate within the broader culture.

Throughout my many years serving within the institutional church, including the years in which I have been ordained, I have often found myself wondering about what it is that motivates people to attend worship on Sunday mornings. Having been raised Roman Catholic, even to the point of attending Catholic school in the pre-Vatican II years, I have understood the hold that church laws have had on the conscience and behavior of Catholics of my generation. When I began worshiping at and eventually preparing for ordination within the framework of Protestantism, I found myself both fascinated and amazed with the fact that so many people in Protestant churches with which I had contact would attend worship regularly, even though unlike the Catholics among whom I was raised, there was no law within their churches requiring them to do so under penalty of mortal or at least venial sin. As many of you reading this know, the Catholic Church has a long-standing legal tradition, i.e., holding to a compilation of laws expected to be binding upon the faithful Roman Catholic under penalty of sin.

Therefore, with this contrast very much in mind, the question of motivation is one about which I have often wondered. I have found myself thinking: What is the driving force that compels people to be part of worship, even though, technically speaking, they were not *required* to attend?

Of course, all the statistical indicators show that over these past few years there has been considerable decline in attendance within mainline Protestant churches. Perhaps that very fact provided the answer I needed to that question. Anecdotal evidence provided me in various conversations over the course of time I have spent as a Protestant pastor led me to think that an important factor in this decline is that, for some reason or other, it has become acceptable within these church communities for people to attend less frequently and often more sporadically than used to be the case. *In fact, the acceptable reasons for absence may have broadened from where they were decades or even years ago. This might include youth participation in athletic events, the opportunities for families to spend time traveling, even if that meant going on Sunday morning day trips or even the possibility of getting some well needed sleep or grocery or other shopping out of the way before one entered a frantic work week!* While recent church attendance has been altered due to all the health concerns emerging from COVID-19[8], the fact remains that this decline in church attendance was in full swing before the pandemic hit!

When we examine it closely, we can see that the reality of the institutional church is that a great deal of emphasis is placed on the following:

- Caring for the church building and raising the necessary funds to do so.
- Directing much of church leadership in the direction of making wise decisions that help support the upkeep of the church building. Consequently, a good deal of conversation at council meetings and business gatherings of the local church is centered on items such as the heater, air conditioning costs, maintenance of the roof, etc. It is important to state that the upkeep of the building is very important. However, meetings of lay persons engaged in church leadership easily move in the direction of prioritizing issues and the decisions to be made regarding them. What I have found over the years is that less time at these meetings is spent discussing questions related to the underlying nature and mission of the church. This includes a lack of focus on such things as the poverty and hunger to be found in the neighborhood or community in which the church resides OR perhaps in the dearth of opportunities available for young people in the church's contiguous neighborhoods and what the church might be able to do to bring about some needed change!

    *Again, to be clear, building maintenance **is** important. However, a church council needs to be deeply engaged in questions related to such matters as service to others and offering the church it serves opportunities to put the Gospel of Jesus into practice.*

- Offering activities of interest to the membership of the church. Usually these are not centered on programs of Christian Education or social outreach. Instead, they take on the form of tag sales, church suppers,

---

8. The coronavirus which began affecting countries throughout the world in 2020 and remains active at the time of this writing.

holiday fairs, movie or bingo nights and other 'social' activities. It is important to acknowledge that *these kinds of activities are helpful in terms of building and reinforcing bonds among the members and friends of the congregation. They may also stir up interest among those not involved in church life. I am most certainly not in favor of eliminating them from a church's agenda!*

However, in examining these areas of interest for the leadership of the local church, here are some areas that can be absent from conversation or given lesser priority:

- Developing social outreach initiatives that can engage the members and friends of the church, including those of a wide range of ages.
- Offering programs where one would invite members of the local and surrounding communities which are directed toward supporting important causes centered on social outreach. From personal experience, I would suggest, among other options, benefit concerts, with benefit money going to a worthwhile cause, as a wonderful way of making the church's presence known within the communities surrounding it and in making a statement that the church is not simply an in-house operation but a gathering of people attuned to real life needs within the area, nation and world.

One memorable example of this occurred when I was serving as a church pastor at the time the Flint, Michigan water crisis struck. Having learned that a local church in Flint affiliated with our denomination was actively engaged in helping those who were suffering from the horrific problems surrounding this water, our church, led by the young people in it, sponsored a concert featuring a well-known singer in our state, a woman with a deep passion for issues of social justice. The result was:

- A wonderful concert
- A significant amount of money raised for a good cause
- The presence of many people in attendance who had no connection to our church but were able to witness the reality that this is not a church focused only on itself

As a rule, and, in my old age, I will concede to some limited exceptions. It strikes me as of paramount importance that when a church plans a benefit concert or any other similar event, the best possible focus is outward, as opposed to a benefit that is directed toward raising funds to pay for the boiler, air conditioning, roof or other similar causes. In my experience, I have found that the tendency of many churches is to use special events to raise money for themselves.

To be clear, I am *not* saying that a church should never raise money to keep the building warm or appropriately cool nor to take steps to keep the facility intact. What I *am* saying is that in terms of broader community witness and presence, a church engaging in fund raising which leads to true service to others sends a message which is outright evangelical in nature, i.e., a message about the core values of the Gospel, reflected in Matthew 25, a passage to which we will return throughout this book:

> [31] "When the Son of Man comes in his glory, and all the angels with him, then he will sit on the throne of his glory. [32] All the nations will be gathered before him, and he will separate people one from another as a shepherd separates the sheep from the goats, [33] and he will put the sheep at his right hand and the goats at the left. [34] Then the king will say to those at his right hand, 'Come, you that are blessed by my Father, inherit the kingdom prepared for you from the foundation of the world; [35] for I was hungry and you gave me food, I was thirsty and you gave me something to drink, I was a stranger and you welcomed me, [36] I was naked and you gave me clothing, I was sick and you took care of me, I was in prison and you visited me.' [37] Then the righteous will answer him, 'Lord, when was it that we saw you hungry and gave you food, or thirsty and gave you something to drink? [38] And when was it that we saw you a stranger and welcomed you, or naked and gave you clothing? [39] And when was it that we saw you sick or in prison and visited you?' [40] And the king will answer them, 'Truly I tell you, just as you did it to one of the least of these who are members of my family,[a] you did it to me.' [41] Then he will say to those at his left hand, 'You that are accursed, depart from me into the eternal fire prepared for the devil and his angels; [42] for I was hungry and you gave me no food, I was thirsty and you gave me nothing to drink, [43] I was a stranger and you did not welcome me, naked and you did not give me clothing, sick and in prison and you did not visit me.' [44] Then they also will answer, 'Lord, when was it that we saw you hungry or thirsty or a stranger or naked or sick or in prison, and did not take care of you?' [45] Then he will answer them, 'Truly I tell you, just as you did not do it to one of the least of

these, you did not do it to me.' ⁴⁶ *And these will go away into eternal punishment, but the righteous into eternal life."*⁹

If one were to think in terms of a so-called marketing strategy i.e., what might attract people to a church, a community of faith that conveys the following characteristics would most definitely have the upper hand in comparison to a church that functions simply with business as usual:

- Energy
- Innovation
- Outreach to those beyond the walls of the church
- An interest in engaging a broad spectrum of people and ideas
- A willingness to think outside of the box
- An understanding that what attracts people to a church in these early stages of the 21st century is different from what may have done so in the heydays of the century prior!
- A sense that people need to find meaning and purpose in what happens on Sunday morning or any other time the church gathers for worship. Meaningful worship is central to the life of a church! It is not enough to be a participant out of some sense of mere obligation!

THE IMPORTANCE OF SELF-AWARENESS . . .

I have learned over the years that it is important every now and then for a church to stop and take a pause. This includes examining who and what the church *is right now, at this point in time!* Using as an example the most recent congregation I have served, I will attempt to make the point of that it is essential for a church to be profoundly self-aware. As I look at the demographics and dynamics of this congregation, I see a picture of a church not at all unlike others where I have been pastoring over these last few years. In presenting this picture, I want to be clear that there is NO criticism of this church even remotely implied. Rather my focus is on some basic facts:

- Were you to walk into worship on a Sunday morning, the majority of participants would be at least 60 years old or older (including its pastor!!)

9. Matthew 25:31–46

- Were you to walk in, you would most likely see very few children, young people or young adults in attendance. Here is where it is important to state that in some larger churches, you probably would find a higher number of young people. This might be because with more adults attending, there would likewise be the possibility of children as part of the overall family unit. Nonetheless, in relation to the potential number of children in the local geographic area, the likelihood is that the number participating is quite low.

- Were you to come by and listen to the announcements offered by members of the congregation, you would find that people in this church look forward to a variety of fun activities throughout the year that raise money for the church. This church has had excellent financial success offering tag sales, holiday fairs and has recently ventured into a fun filled creative approach to trivia!

- You would also find that the money taken in from these events goes toward money needed for the church to meet its financial obligations.

- You would notice as well that this church makes sure to go out of its way to support such worthwhile programs as Relay for Life (American Cancer Society) or an annual walk to benefit those programs supporting individuals with disabilities and special needs.

- You would discover that a monthly offering is taken up to assist a variety of programs in the community as well as those supported by the church's denomination.

All these initiatives mentioned above are good and worthy of commendation.

However, when you look back at the first bullet point, what is quite clear is that the age demographic indicates that unless there is an increase in church participation and membership over a narrow period, there will be a natural attrition in the number of people who will be part of this church. As was the case over a recent two-and-a-half-year period, there will be decreases in membership and church participation because of illness, death or people moving out of town, often moving away at a considerable distance. On the plus side of this is that, thanks to a good online presence, several members of the congregation who have moved away remain connected by watching services and other programs on the church's Facebook page and via other means that the church has developed.

Where There Is Hatred, Love

Now, one of the positives in this congregation has been that over a relatively brief period, the church has taken in many new members. These members have tended to come from this same demographic, primarily centered around individuals close to or already at retirement age. Within this church, the children and youth you will see come primarily from two family groups. These families are deeply committed to and wonderfully involved in this church!

While at the time of this writing, I have left this church as pastor not because of any negatives involved but rather due to the fact that I have been quite busy over an almost 45 year period as an educator, counselor, coach and pastor and I decided that it is time to move into the phase of life known as retirement, I am most pleased that even during the time of the COVID-19 pandemic, people in the church remained connected to each other and we had an incredible spirit of volunteerism which was so helpful and necessary in keeping this church intact and active. We did a lot of groundbreaking work utilizing technological options for both worship and online educational programs!

However, what we were impeded from doing because of this pandemic was to offer opportunities which might engage a broader number of people within our surrounding communities. We never got to hold the concert that I hoped we would with the money raised for it going to a worthwhile cause outside of the church and providing the possibility of bringing into the church building people of different ages. We were not able to schedule a return benefit opportunity for Simply Smiles [10]*or to engage that organization in presenting young people in our area with the service opportunities they could have alongside youth from other churches. In addition, we were unable to have the ecumenical youth night scheduled to be held on the weekend the pandemic first shut things down in 2020, an event that would affirm the potential for young people from different churches connecting on behalf of others, even as the wider mainline church has struggled to maintain their youth ministry programs.* [11]

During this time, the church did some things that were important for its ongoing maintenance. At appropriate times, we were able to get tag sales and church fairs up and running to provide needed income for the church.

---

10. A wonderful organization which helps meet the needs of children who live on the Cheyenne River reservation in South Dakota, as well as children living in the area of Oaxaca, Mexico.

11. A concern of mine is the decline in Youth Ministry programs in mainline churches.

We were successful in getting PPP loans[12] due to the hard work of several of our committed church members. Our church was readied for worship and kept in great shape by a dedicated team of volunteers. Somehow, amid a chaotic, change-filled time, we had a new roof put in. These were wonderful and necessary things.

Yet, as I told the church gathered on the day I preached for the final time as their pastor, how I wished we were able to have that youth event and for those kids to have had the chance to do more in the communities beyond the church's walls! I have often thought of what we might have done *on behalf of others, perhaps even with the possibility that some of those others, of different ages, might have found themselves excited about connecting with the nature and the mission of this church!*

You see, one of the things I *love* the most about the church is its potential to engage and energize people with a vision of what the Gospel message of Jesus can be like when it is really put into practice. In other words, there is an incredible vibrancy to be found in a church that has an outward focused mission consciousness. *Though I struggle with some of the causes advocated by some of the more conservative churches, including those of the megachurch variety, I commend them for offering opportunities for service to people outside the walls of that church.* Several of these churches are very successful in terms of direct outreach and helping people with basic needs. My quarrel is with much of the theology that is taught within these churches and that is shared with those participating in worship at them. *However, to be honest, what I really hate is whatever churches do that lead to the perception of those who are not connected to them that they are driven only by internal interests and are looking for ways to raise money primarily to take care of those items that, in and of themselves,* do not *constitute the mission of the church.* In wrapping up this chapter, it is important that I make myself clear:

A church needs income to function. In winter in cold climates, a building needs to be heated. Those working in churches deserve fair and just salaries and the property must be maintained. However, the mission of the church is centered on the Gospel of Jesus and carries with it an underlying question:

What are we, those who are part of this community called church, to do to carry out the work of Jesus in the community in which we exist and how are we to bear witness that the church of Jesus Christ exists to serve the broader world beyond its walls as well?

---

12. Government loans made available during the pandemic

3

The Local Church

The world of the relatively early 21st century is a very busy world! With this hectic pace dominating the lifestyles of those of us young, old, or in between, it is fair to ask what the potential benefits would be in being part of a local church community. *What would be the incentives for attending worship or affiliating with a church?* One could contend quite fairly that in the fast-paced modern world, one of the things people need most is some time for relaxation and recreation. Already committed to many responsibilities, why should one even think about adding more? One of the few places people find either those opportunities or the extra time to do some required tasks, such as shopping or tending to one's house, might very well be on a Sunday morning, a time ordinarily set aside for going to services of worship.

Now, within this context, we find another reality: In a busy world, where people have job and family responsibilities, even were one to attend worship, what is the possibility that a person might find the time to engage in any positions of leadership within that congregation? For a very long time, there have also been a variety of different roles one who belongs to a local church might play. Some acted as regular churchgoers, people for whom consistent church attendance on Sundays and other special days was part of their lifestyle. For those with children, these young people also were integrated appropriately into church life by attendance at Sunday School, CCD sacramental preparation classes, confirmation programs and the like with their parents or parents of some of their friends often involved in teaching in those classes and programs. Youth connected with churches have had opportunities to engage with other youth through church designed youth group programming, appropriate at various age levels.

What we are seeing in recent years is that a greater number of people than ever are holding back from assuming positions on such bodies as church council or other important church committees. We are seeing this at a time when mainline church attendance is facing considerable decline. This is a reality that churches need to face. Oftentimes, we see that people who do not really enjoy serving in leadership positions nonetheless volunteer to do so because of their deep commitment to the church. This is commendable. However, we also find that these people are likewise susceptible to becoming frustrated and burned out as these responsibilities often do not *play to their strengths.* My suggestion is that churches face this reality by asking this question: *What is necessary for the local church to function well?* Now, to be honest, this is a loaded question! While I am not suggesting that I am providing the reader the ideal or perfect answers, my intention here is to make some suggestions for the reader to consider. These necessities are not listed in order of importance. It is also possible that one reading this could suggest in response to my writing that I have left a few important things out. I hope not, but it *is* possible! At any rate, to the question of necessity, i.e., those things necessary for a local church to be functioning well, I would suggest consideration of the following:

- The church needs to make a commitment to meaningful worship and preaching. This includes serious attention to the ways in which music is used within the context of worship. *I would suggest that a church show a willingness to expose those attending worship to the variety of musical styles available within the broader category of music for worship.* I have learned over the years that, even when churches have one of the latest available published hymnals sitting in their pew racks week in and week out, in the selection of weekly hymns, you will find that the church sings a very small number of them. I have had experiences where church members and friends have told me how excited they were to hear a new hymn sung at worship on a particular morning, a hymn that very well may have been written 30 or 40 years ago and has been an important part of that denomination's history! *Likewise, it is important to note that in the last few decades, there has been considerable crossover in church music. In other words, hymns that would appear solely in Protestant hymnals have found their way into Catholic ones and vice versa.* In addition, many churches simply do not keep up with updated hymnals published by their denomination or with new music that is available from many sources within the Christian tradition. As a result, oftentimes people in one tradition are surprised, shocked or in dismay when they are at a church service and hear a hymn played and sung that is from a church tradition different from their own. In my view, the onus for dealing with this rests with the pastor who bears the responsibility to keep up with the latest trends in music for worship! Ideally, in a church with a music director, the pastor and director would work collaboratively[1].

I encountered this reality that oftentimes churches do not keep up with church music about 30 years ago when I was a Catholic deacon and was responsible for presiding at the marriage of a young couple. The young man getting married was raised in the Baptist tradition and his wife to be a Roman Catholic. He asked me if we could have a special song at the wedding, one that was his grandmother's favorite and that she used to sing while walking around and cleaning the house. The hymn he requested was *'Just a Closer Walk with Thee'*[2], a favorite hymn in many churches, primarily Protestant ones at that time. I assured him that we could but then the very traditionally oriented organist at that Catholic church told me she could not do it because it was a so-called 'Protestant' hymn. When my objection and the fact that I was ultimately responsible for this church service did not persuade her, I appealed to the pastor, and he acceded to my request. *Fortunately, the reality is that if one were to look in the hymn books of many Protestant denominations these days, one would find many hymns originally composed for Catholic worship. On the flip side, one would find an awful lot of hymns in Catholic publications that have been embraced as favorites by Protestants.* In fact, on several occasions in a church in the United Church of Christ which I served as pastor for 11 ½ years, we would have a service where people could request many hymns as part of worship. Among the top 10 selected over time, 4 of those happened to be hymns originally from the Roman Catholic tradition!

- Engaged leadership of both lay persons and clergy and staff. *Here it is important to acknowledge that the expectations for those who are paid*

---

1. Here is where I have been most fortunate to have had such collaborative relationships with church musicians in congregations that I have served!
2. A traditional gospel song.

for their services (e.g., pastor, Christian education director, youth minister, musician, etc. . . .) should be different from those who volunteer. However, it is also important to strive for a church community which encourages and supports a passion for volunteerism. In fact, ideally, one would hope for those willing to volunteer that they explore finding ways to serve the church within their areas of interest!

- An outward service focus. A group of individuals formed for the purpose of living the message of Jesus needs to take on tasks which are *outwardly directed*. This is crucial. Apart from being the right thing to do, this also is appealing to those who seek to apply their Christian values in real, practical, service-oriented ways.

- An attentiveness to the importance of *music* within the church community, not necessarily limited to worship but also available in concerts and possibly theatrical productions. This point is spelled out in the comments I have made above!

A model for this is found in the volunteer experiences within the broader society. For example, young boys and girls who are interested in specific sports benefit from those adults who are willing to parlay their own interests in, for example baseball or soccer, and provide a good, positive experience for youth. *That model can readily be applied to the church and how it approaches volunteerism. Wouldn't it be great if churches could have volunteers filled with passion and enthusiasm for a variety of positive ventures?*

While, over the years, many churches have expended time and energy in providing social opportunities for members, we also need to recognize that the times have changed in many ways. *Churches are no longer the centers of social activity as they once were.* People have discovered many different means of participating in activities that they enjoy. Consequently, it is quite possible that many church activities which used to be big draws are not quite as attractive anymore. *This reflects the reality that the church no longer functions as the center of social life.* I say this with the understanding that in some communities, the local church does remain the center of activity. However, that reality is clearly dwindling, as are the number of long-established churches in many of those communities.

Nonetheless, this situation is not something to bemoan. Instead, churches need to explore new ways of engaging people. This engagement is best when it is consistent with the church's mission. For example, a church concert or tag sale wherein money would go to a worthwhile cause within the community, or the broader society might very well have great appeal to those not connected with church but who want to do something valuable for others. *In fact, it strikes me that an important responsibility of the church is to help people tap into the good that is very much present within them and help them discover ways to put it into practice.*

One of the best indicators of a vibrant church in the current context is of one which is deeply engaged in the community beyond its walls. This represents a shift from how church activities were often advertised in those days when church life was an integral part of the lives of so many. As an example, I would give the annual tradition of a church fair, known as the *Circle of Fun,* in my home parish of my childhood days. Apart from having a good time, people attending this Fair tended to be tuned in to the importance of raising money for the church and the church's elementary school. Many people in my predominantly French Canadian Roman Catholic community saw that cause as one that was worthwhile. Within our contemporary society, the cause of Catholic education within local parishes and communities is not really on the radar screen anymore. However, there are other pressing social needs in local communities to which churches could make positive contributions.

What I am suggesting is that churches shift from an inner focus to one that is directed outward. While all indicators show that there *is* a decline in peoples' connections to local churches as represented in attendance figures, the wonderful reality still exists that people *do* care about giving to those in need. This is demonstrated in so many ways, oftentimes in fund raising drives or *Go Fund Me* [3] initiatives, contributions for specific causes that stir peoples' hearts, as well as in food drives throughout the year.

In a day and age where ties to the local church are not what they used to be, the appeal to pay for the church's heating system or to put in air conditioning is limited. In fact, the appeal is primarily internal. In other words, the regular church goer would look at her/his experience in that church building and be convinced of the importance of these kinds of changes. Now, please do not misunderstand me, ok? A church must and should keep its building in good shape. *However, the shift that needs to be made is one that moves from a focus on the church's internal needs to that which is more outward driven, and which considers the community beyond the church's walls.*

---

3. An online resource which people can use to make donations to worthwhile causes.

Now, here is where I think I really need to make something, as one might say, perfectly clear:

For a person whom one might call a church insider, i.e., someone who is actively engaged in doing volunteer work around the church, there might very well be considerable appeal in campaigns designed to keep the building running well, bringing in income for needed repairs, taking care of the furnace, etc. Yet, the available evidence makes clear that the overwhelming majority in any local town or suburb or any neighborhood within a city really, to use a colloquialism, "really could not give a hoot" about the boiler problem in the neighborhood church on the corner. Simply put: Short of attending funerals in the building, most local folks go many years, some an entire lifetime, without walking into some of the churches in their community or neighborhood.

Now, this is not to say that the problem should be taken lightly because a church might very well need heat come the cold winter months. It is to say, however, that this issue is not really an issue to someone who looks at the church from the outside. In fact, it might not even mean very much to one who attends worship at this church and is more interested in what the church can do to serve the needs of others than she/he might be in taking care of practical, technical problems.

In fact, from my experience, there has been less interest among young adults in building issues than there has been in the kinds of programs a church might offer its youth. Among busy people for whom the idea of church is viable, it is fair to say that there is more passion for putting faith into practice and engaging youth in worthwhile activities that are expressive of that faith than there is in some of the internal building questions which inevitably will impact any church which owns its own building, a building it calls church, often despite the fact that *a church is really not a building!*

Here is where I would like to offer some specific suggestions. In offering them, I also wish to acknowledge that, in the same way that all politics is local[4] these need to be examined in the context of the specific church which one is discussing. In other words, these are not one size fits all recommendations. Having said that, I would suggest that reflecting on them could be a good starting point for examination of what might be best for a local church:

---

4. A phrase popularized by Tip O' Neill, former Speaker of the United States House of Representatives.

The Local Church

1. No matter how many changes in leadership format a church develops, there is a need for consistency. In other words, you will need people within churches who hold positions that have some reasonable degree of length. Consequently, a church council, elected by membership, is important within the local church.

2. Be attentive to burnout. It is natural for people to get frustrated if they feel they are doing all the work. This frustration ends up being quite counterproductive.

3. Decentralize responsibilities. *Not everyone doing things within the church has to hold an official leadership title.* For example, someone with artistic talent may be able to take those talents and use them to make significant, creative impact upon the inner design of the church. He/she may have no interest in attending a bunch of council meetings, but, most definitively, has talents to share. A person might have great gifts working with children or teens or visiting the homebound but finds attendance at committee meetings an inadequate use of her/his time. Churches need to encourage people to use their gifts and strengths and provide opportunities for them to do so!

4. It is important to expand the concept of leadership. It should not mean only elected leadership.

5. Help people make the shift to short term commitments in terms of exploring options for service as a member or friend of the church.

6. Work toward getting all engaged in some way, not all necessarily over the same time.

7. *Create a ministry sense.* This is the greatest challenge. From the pulpit and through other ways of communicating, it is important to help people grasp and perceive the reality that an outgrowth of their presence in the church community means that they are, in fact, ministers. Here is where the concept of the priesthood of believers has significant practical implications. Even in this, the 21st century, there remains a tendency to identify 'ministry' with the work of the person who is ordained. The church needs to move beyond this. Church members need to be aided in processing the concept of ministry. It is important to get people to reflect on the ways they minister and to take a close look at the ministry activity of the pastor. It is crucial that they learn to see that *the pastor is not the only minister in the congregation.* In my early

days transitioning from the Roman Catholic Church, I found myself astonished that in conversations with church members, I would often hear the word *minister* used in conversations as referring only to the one who served as pastor. It is important to have a broader definition!

8. Explore innovative, creative ways to save money in the use of one's building. In some cases, this could include using a different worship space within the building during those winter days when a building may need to be heated. One might consider whether it would be frugal to heat a sanctuary which seats 200 people when in fact, only 30 or 40 might be expected to attend worship. The use of a smaller space within the building could both save money and provide a meaningful setting for worship. This also offers great possibilities for members and friends of the congregation to use creative talents to design the worship space.

9. *Though many would find this suggestion troublesome, I would suggest deemphasizing the concept of membership within a church.* While this is not the same as abolishing it, it would send out a very different message from what one might find in the traditional translation of the word member. Over the years, I have seen many people be actively involved in their church who, for one reason or another, did not see belonging as a member as a necessity. From my perspective, while I would suggest to those interested in church participation that membership is a good thing and I would encourage people to consider affirming membership in the presence of the church, I also believe quite strongly that one can be deeply engaged in a church's mission without holding the formal title of member. In speaking to church participants, I have always tended to refer to *all who are part of our church community as opposed to singling out those who are members. This is one of those areas where tradition is strong and would be difficult to break from for many.* Having said that, I think it is worth thinking through!

UNDERLYING REALITY

It is crucial that we frame this discussion within the context of an incontrovertible fact, one based in extensive research of trends in religion in our nation. *Current research indicates that 31.3% of the American population has no religious affiliation.*[5] Mainline Protestantism and Roman Catholicism have shown massive declines over the last several years. While we can look at the data and crunch the numbers, I also wish to offer some observations from personal experience:

I have been an ordained clergyperson for 33 years, as of this writing. During that time frame, I have seen significant changes, many of which were in the embryonic stage when I began my ordained ministry. When I was training for ministry and when I first began, I found that when I participated in a funeral or a wedding, a rather good number of people present had some familiarity with the prayer rituals attached to each event. Even though Protestants at Catholic funerals may not have known some of the prayers and gestures of the ritual, there was a lot within the ceremony which was quite familiar. I saw that from Catholics at Protestant services as well, some even expressing that they were surprised that these services had so much in common.

As my years within the ordained ministry have gone on and piled up, I have seen a change. Though I never pursued gathering statistical data on this, it has been obvious to me experientially that many participants at these services had very little familiarity with the rituals and prayers involved. For better or worse, people who attend worship in a religious tradition with some degree of consistency have at least a rote sense of the prayers being said as well as the overall patterns of the liturgical actions. People in funeral homes or at gravesites would often instinctively pray along with Psalm 23 or have a built-in response mechanism pointing them in the direction of making the Sign of the Cross.

Over these last few years, I have found that this familiarity is fading. In fact, I have also discovered that when I use this religious language, I also need to accompany it with some brief explaining and/or translating. When I use this term translating, I am referring to the reality that much of what passes as religious language does not resonate with many people who are hearing it. That does not mean that the language itself is therefore meaningless. Instead, it indicates an absence of familiarity and knowledge of some of the terminology found in Biblical passages or church developed traditional prayers. Now, of course, another issue here is that for many, probably most, people raised within churches, their study of religious documents such as the Bible was really limited to a few years in their lives, usually ending sometime during adolescence. In fact, many professors at Catholic

---

5. See Burge, *The Nones*.

and mainline Protestant affiliated colleges will claim that a good number of their students come from a very limited theological background.

In my view, this translating is therefore most crucial. As one example, I would note the fact that many people I have met at graveside services do not have ongoing connection with church communities. *What is important in those situations is that the person officiating provide a meaningful experience, religious in nature. This might include basic explanations of what is being said in certain prayers and Scripture readings, doing so in a direct way, which can connect with the reality of the emotions people are currently experiencing. Another way of saying this is that one should do so in a non-robotic way, attuned to the best ways this message can be presented to those not currently familiar with much of church ritualistic practice. One might even consider exploring ways of expressing spirituality which are not bound to a robotic style of traditional worship. This involves considerable self-reflection of the person officiating with an accompanying awareness of the tendency to fall back on the usual language and phraseology of liturgy.*

Some might contend that this is oversimplification or disregard for sacred texts and worship formats, but I would argue that it is not. After all, when one is confronted, for example with the experience of mourning a death, even if one does not have a theological handle on all the prayers and Bible passages available within the ritual, it is fair to say that one does have a sense of the mysteries inherent in life, death, eternity, and love, all of which are confronted as part of the rituals of religious groups. However, the key is to move away from rote ritual and to adapt these experiences in ways that tap into the real life experience the participants are having.

I am sure that I have led services at gravesites for many people who, in mourning the loss of their beloved, have not, through their lives, been absorbed in conversations or study regarding different perspectives on what happens after one dies. However, when one is at the grave of someone who has been very special in one's life, a person may naturally and instinctively call to mind the experiences she/he has had with that person and the ways in which that deceased person's life has had meaning and purpose. *What I am saying is that experiences of death, commitment in love and new birth, all celebrated within the rituals or sacraments of churches contain moments of profound, deep reflection.* In the questions running through peoples' minds are matters of ultimate importance and of deep mystery. Way down deep, even for those who have not set foot inside of a church for years, there are questions about the mystery taking place before and around them. Even when not verbalized in official church language, the big questions are there-about God, afterlife, love and so much more . . .

The writer James Carroll, one of my favorites, describes this well in a very powerful essay he wrote a few years back in which *he makes clear that we cannot fully comprehend the reality and the mystery of God.* I would add that the way in which God is all too often presented, i.e., as a doctrine one is obliged to follow really gets in the way of getting a sense of what God might possibly be all about. Here is what Carroll says:

"The God to whom Jesus points is the God beyond "God." We recognize in Jesus all that we need to know about the God who, otherwise, remains incomprehensible. And this recognition, because well rooted in the past, is powerful enough to carry us into the open-ended future, even extending beyond what can be imagined.[6]*"*

In noting the incomprehensibility of God, Carroll does an extremely important thing: *He points us in the direction of honestly acknowledging that God is mystery.* In my view, it is important that we affirm this sense of mystery. *This should lead us all to profound respect for those outside of the Christian tradition who seek to live their lives in relationship to the divine. Likewise, this recognition of God as mystery should open our hearts as well to those troubled by the interpretations many people in traditional religions have made about God's characteristics and intentions.* Drawing on resources of other theologians and his own experience Carroll offers an insight that put into practice, can help translate churchy language in ways that make sense to those contemporaries not tuned into a working knowledge of this kind of language. In essence, Carroll conveys a simple message: *God's a mystery but if you want to get a sense of God, look at Jesus!* To be clear, this does not mean that God is dressed up as Jesus. From my perspective, I see Jesus' life as providing those around him with the experience of God's compassion, love, presence and so much more! In addition, his life provides us with that possible experience as well, if we confront that life with open minds and hearts, unencumbered by doctrinal and liturgical language which can act as an impediment to that possibility.

This process of **looking to Jesus** *is one that must be done very carefully. It is not an approach that calls for what we might call a doctrinal interpretation. What am I saying? Looking to Jesus does not mean that we run immediately in the direction of defining Jesus or offering doctrines about him. It is not*

---

6. "Who is Jesus Today?", a talk presented by James Carroll and published in the Harvard Divinity School bulletin, Summer/Autumn, 2014.

about limiting Jesus to the confines of the language used in official creeds of the institutional church. Instead, it is about focusing in on Jesus' words spoken to others and, equally significantly, about getting a sense of his actions. In the poet's words, we would do so with the recognition that 'Christ' plays in 10,000 places, lovely in . . . eyes not His . . . [7]

While more conservative Christian churches place focus on specific doctrines about Jesus and look at the relationship between following Jesus and attaining salvation, the focus I am describing, without denying doctrine or the value of salvation, looks at the actions Jesus lived out in His life and how they serve as examples for us. Yet, I would contend that even more than the examples they set, in them we are able to catch a glimpse of the divine, i.e., to catch a glimpse of God. If we look closely at the Gospels, we will find this man Jesus engaged in the process of coming to terms with himself. We see this in the story we find in Luke's Gospel where Jesus reads a passage from Isaiah in his hometown synagogue and then pauses to give the message that "this day, this passage is being fulfilled in your hearing[8]" This is quite a powerful message, don't you think?

I would contend that in this way of talking and teaching about Jesus the church needs to place focus on the importance of discipleship. What do I mean? It seems to me that a local church that focuses on energizing people to find ways to serve others and that deliberately concentrates outward towards the needs of others is a church that is both faithful to the core values of Christianity and which has great appeal to those who seek to find meaning in purpose in being part of this institution.

It strikes me that within the world of those who were raised in the church, there are varied degrees of relationship to it. I cite three examples:

1. *Those for whom the church is an integral part of their lives and serving within it in some way (or at least contributing to it) is important to them.*

2. *Those for whom connection with the church was part of their past but not terribly relevant in the present moment on a day-to-day basis. This is not to say that they are not spiritual people. It is simply to say that the institution does not do much for them, for varied, sundry reasons.*

And there is a third one that is exciting:

7. Hopkins poem cited previously
8. Luke 4:21

The Local Church

3. *Those, not limited to the young but perhaps inspired by them, who see Christianity as something to put into practice through real life actions.* **You could call this a Matthew 25 approach to Christianity.** *It is an approach to faith that involves the practical application of words such as these: "When I was hungry, you gave me to eat . . . thirsty and you gave me to drink. 'It is a Christianity inspired by not only the words of Jesus but the ways in which He put them into practice.*

There are many powerful examples to be found within the Bible:

- *You see this not only in Matthew 25 but in the poignant story of the woman at the well. (John 4)*
- *You see it when Jesus confronts the crowd that was readying to stone the so-called sinful woman (John 8:1–11)*
- *You see it in the parable of the Prodigal Son (Luke 15:11–46)*
- *You will find it in the story of the Samaritan called good. (Luke 10:25–37)*

As I have mentioned previously, during the time in which I have been writing this book, the church I serve held a Confirmation service on a Pentecost Sunday. While my sermon was prepared in advance, I tried to deliver it in a way wherein it would lend itself to some spontaneity. It was important to me on that day that I speak directly to the two young women who were being confirmed and veer away from a text dependent only upon words I had already typed. Having spent many a year working in youth ministry, one of my great concerns about congregational life is about how young people feel they fit in. In addition, my experience in churches has been that for many of us older church goers, there is somewhat of a discrepancy between our perceptions of church when we were young and that of a more contemporary generation. What I learned from looking at the billboard one of my high school teachers was a lesson I carried through my life. When it comes to religion, people, be they young or old, need to find *meaning and relevance.*[9]

For older folks (and I fit in this category, as I am close to 70 at the time of this writing), church back then was a place that met many of our social needs. The world is different now with cell phones, tweeting, texting, and all kinds of different means available for young people to bond together

---

9. I am referring to the bulletin board in the classroom of one of my high school teachers, the late Mr. Sean Drury. There will be more about him later on in this chapter!

socially. While the pandemic[10] has demonstrated the gap in one's personal life caused by isolation, for sure, nevertheless in so called ordinary times, it is fair to say that young people do have opportunities for social interaction that are quite appealing which happen not to be centered on the church.

In addition, the parents of these youth come from a generation which, for various and sundry reasons, had major declines in church attendance in their teenage years, in comparison with that of generations before them. Back when I was young, so to speak, Protestant and Catholics in my small town spent considerable Sunday mornings at their respective churches. For a multiplicity of reasons, such is not the case for many of the parents of this generation.

This reality first struck me when I served as a director of religious education and youth minister in some Catholic parishes before I was ordained a clergyperson in the Protestant tradition. As a director of religious education, I was responsible for preparing young people for Communion and Confirmation. My work as a youth minister also involved a great deal of responsibility helping students understand what it might mean to them should they opt to choose to be confirmed. While attendance for youth (and their parents at times) was required as part of the process, there were significant declines in parental and family worship attendance in the years between the reception of First Communion and Confirmation. Of course, skillful leaders found ways of building in some special requirements so that parents and children would show up on occasion but the tendency of many of the 1980's and 1990's parents in those churches was toward holding their children to the minimum requirements connected with the process of receiving these sacraments of the church.

When I entered life as a Protestant and began working with youth, I noticed a similar reality taking place in the process of Confirmation preparation. What I realized from both my Protestant and Catholic experiences in leadership was that there was clearly a decline in commitment to worship attendance come Sundays in comparison to the time in which I grew up,

I tell you all of this to let you in on my mindset on that Pentecost morning when I delivered a sermon to two wonderful young teenage women who were about to be confirmed. In what may have come across as off the cuff remarks because I was not operating off a written sermon text in front of me, yet what was a message I prepared very carefully, I tried to communicate to these girls that the heart, soul and core of Christian faith,

---

10. COVID 19

The Local Church

this faith they were affirming, was Jesus. I encouraged them to get into their Bibles and look, really look, at all those situations when Jesus did what we might call some radical things.

Anyone listening who has a touch of the love for traditional institutional religion might have felt I was really criticizing organized religion as it is. I most clearly was quite dismissive of an approach to Christianity centered on fancy buildings as well as traditions often misunderstood, poorly explained and sometimes even downright irrelevant. In effect, I told these girls to read about Jesus and to zero in on his amazingly radical thoughts and actions.

Now, any intelligent person reading about Jesus and coming across what He really said, did and emphasized, must be taken aback a bit. Consider these words and actions of Jesus as recorded in the Gospels:

- He threw a temper tantrum when he overturned tables in a place considered to be sacred space for worship.
- He broke religious laws on the holiest of days of the week and provided a rationale for what He did.
- He called the despised, discriminated against Samaritan good.
- He told people about to stone an adulterous woman to put down those rocks and look within, unless they were so sinless that they had the right to cast a stone.

Without dismissing or challenging the teachings expressed in the catechisms and formulated for liturgy such as what we find in the Apostles and Nicene Creeds, I tried to make the point that what this faith is all about really starts and ends with Jesus and what He taught and how He lived. Of course, it is from reflection on the reality of these actions of Jesus that the church universal has developed creeds and doctrines which have been crafted in language reflecting the cultures that produced them, but the point remains that at the core of Christianity is the life and activity of Jesus of Nazareth.

Consequently, the life of a Christian, be one a 15-year-old or 70-year-old follower of Jesus, is to be precisely that, a disciple. Therefore, the work of the local church consists of both helping to form disciples, regardless of their age and to engage in lives that reflect a commitment to discipleship i.e., toward following Jesus.

I would contend that this sense of discipleship is something that people feel good about. People really want to find more meaning in belonging to an organization than is often presented by the organization itself. I have seen it firsthand with youth and adults working at homeless shelters or with young people sitting around in a circle on a retreat and talking openly about the struggles they face and being supportive of those who are speaking in their circle.

For young or for old, religious faith is about a search for meaning. When I was a high school, I had a great teacher. Thankfully, I had a lot of good teachers over the years. As I referred to earlier, among the many wonderful things that I remember about Mr. Sean Drury was the bulletin board that was featured in his classroom. Surrounded by pictures of current events in the world outside of that classroom, three simple words stood out in bold lettering, the words *meaningful and relevant*. Mr. Drury bore witness to a faith that he saw as precisely that, a faith that gave people meaning and was deeply connected to their real-life struggles, hopes, dreams, sorrows and joys. This was a man who stood up in a Catholic Church at worship one Sunday to challenge the priest who had made disparaging remarks in his homily about those who leave the priesthood or religious life and opt to get married.[11] I was not there, but when I heard about it, I was quite impressed and wished that I was!

The incentive to be a disciple of Jesus carries with it the recognition that what Jesus taught and how he lived hundreds of years ago in his very short life is *both meaningful and relevant* right now in this place and in this time. It is this incentive that provides the individual an exciting sense of what church is all about. At core, the driving force behind one's participation in this institution called church is the desire for and willingness to live out discipleship, finding in Jesus the values, ethics, and inspiration to live a life filled with meaning and with relevance.

We will explore this in more detail as we go forward to the next chapter but first, let's think about some questions. In concluding this chapter, what I would like to do is suggest that local churches find ways to ask themselves a variety of significant questions. I would encourage pastors and other church leaders give some thought to using these questions at church meetings open to all and focused on the matter of what it really means to be church! Below I have listed some which I consider to be of importance with a suggestion that local churches come up with ones that are relevant

---

11. The words he spoke in challenging the priest who was preaching that day resonated among those of us who knew him and those who were part of this school's life. To the priest in the pulpit, he called out: *"Tell them the real truth"*. Those words became legendary among many of his students and quite inspirational to me!

The Local Church

to their own contexts. Whether it is over coffee or in meaningful meetings, i.e., gatherings in which people of all kinds who are somehow connected to this local church take part, these are questions that could help the local church reflect upon itself and perhaps chart exciting plans for its future:

1. *What is the lure that brings us to this church?*
2. *How does this church compare with other groups to which we belong? To be specific, what does it offer that is unique?*
3. *How does participation in the life of this church affect the life we live in the days when we are not in the church building?*
4. *Does participation in the life of this church lead me to a deeper sense of the value of other people and a deeper sensitivity to issues of justice?*
5. *Does church participation lead me to want to do more in service to others? Does it have an impact in my life as a member of my family and in my workplace.*
6. *Is there anything about this church that leads me to want to recommend it to others?*

4

Church: Social Club or Community of Disciples?

When I think back to my days growing up in the local Catholic Church in my small Connecticut town, my thoughts turn to the memories I have of the involvement that my mother and father had in that local parish in which I was baptized and raised. In many ways, their social life centered on that local church. My parents were regular attendees at church dinners and participated in all kinds of fundraising activities for the local Catholic school which I attended for seven years of my life. They also helped organize special activities for the teenagers with whom they volunteered in the parish's Catholic Youth Organization program, popularly known in Roman Catholic circles as the CYO.

Over the course of a year, they both helped at and enjoyed a variety of social functions. There was an annual spaghetti supper that was a great social activity for most families in the parish. Communion breakfasts on Sunday mornings were a big draw for the men of the church and the women were deeply involved in organizing all kinds of special events and participating in gatherings that brought them together. Support of the parish school led people, male and female alike, to engage in a good amount of fundraising over the course of the year, many of them through events that provided people wonderful opportunities to have a good time! Overall, it is fair to say that the life of the local church offered much of the social life

Church: Social Club or Community of Disciples?

for people of my parents' generation and for younger people such as myself as well.

The remnants of the church as a place for socialization remain within the structure of local churches to this day. However, the realities of the world within and outside of the church have changed. Simply put, the outlets that people in this culture now have for socializing as well as for being entertained have moved way beyond the ways in which people found entertainment and companionship back in the days of my youth. While in some places and contexts, the church does remain the center of activity and social life for people within the community, the fact is that, as a rule, people these days have a wider variety of options for socialization.

In my years growing up, most members of my Catholic parish who had children sent them to the local parish school. That school held a series of events to raise money. These events brought the parents of the community together. It was not unusual to see the same people at the school's fund-raising spaghetti supper on Saturday night who would then be at the 8 am Mass the next morning. While most Protestant congregations in my area did not have schools connected to them, they also exhibited the connection between attendance at their church social events and participation in worship within the congregation. For a while in my latter high school years, I participated in some youth programs at the local Episcopal Church in town. Most of the kids I knew through that program were present in worship each Sunday morning.

In the late 1970's, just before the time when significant changes in local churches began to accelerate at a rapid pace, I coached both the basketball and baseball teams at my local Catholic school, St. Mary's in Putnam, Connecticut. I am pleased to say that over the course of the time I spent as coach, I was fortunate that our teams were supported by in person attendance and financial contributions both by parents and active parishioners who had no children on our teams.

The school's basketball and baseball teams as well as the highly successful traveling football team that was part of the school's not so distant history served the function of providing athletic options to young people within the context of their connection as well as that of their families to the body of the church. In practice, rare were the parents and grandparents of these players who attended their games faithfully who were also not churchgoers on a weekly basis.

I Love the Church, I Hate the Church

Our basketball team was part of a Catholic parochial school league involving teams in my home state of Connecticut as well as ones from over the border in Massachusetts. The allegiance experienced in my home church was something that was quite evident in the other Catholic churches who sponsored teams in that same league. In a different community in which our family resided several years later as our children were growing up, there was a local Interfaith Basketball League which featured teams from local churches and synagogues in that mid-sized community outside of the city of Hartford. By the time our oldest son was in high school, I had opted to explore church options outside of Catholicism and we as a family developed a strong connection with a Lutheran church in that town.

Since my son enjoyed sports, he was interested in playing on the basketball team in this league. As part of that team, he participated along with other young people with the support of that church. In contrast to the situation at St. Mary's about 20 years prior, most of the youth who played on teams sponsored by the local religious institution were not active members of those congregations and, for the most part, neither were their families. The level of local church support was significantly different from what I experienced not that many years before. Over time, this league proved itself to be a relic from an increasingly distant past.

While I am a firm believer that those experiences of being part of a church that engages in special programs as well as sponsoring sports teams has many, many strengths, I also would contend that one must raise a significant question regarding how members of the church perceive themselves. My conviction is that, as valuable as social club experiences might very well be in terms of community building and in seeing church connection as a good, fun experience, *what is most important for local Christians is to be able to identify their local church in terms of discipleship. In other words, the task of those who connect with the church and make it their own is first and foremost that of being disciples of Jesus, individuals seeking to live out the values He taught and exemplified within the community of their local church. Discipleship and social activities need not conflict with one another.* However, if a church's social activities are separate or disconnected from the concept of discipleship, the church simply is not living up to what should be rightfully expected of it!

In my view, there is a strong connection between how we teach the core of Christian faith and how we act it out. Therefore, I believe that it is important for local churches to put significant emphasis on the principle of discipleship. In fact, I would contend that it is important that local churches examine how they perceive themselves. Churches need to explore what they identify as high priorities. As a child growing up within the context I have just described, it was clear to me that local religious institutions offered excellent social opportunities for those who were a part of it. It is from this base of social connection that many churches established what would become long standing traditions in their communities. e.g., church sponsored fairs, barbeques, carnivals, specialty dinners such as the annual spaghetti one in my home parish and the like. These events can and do continue to be positive ones for members of the community.

However, one of the big differences in comparing these days with those of my youth is that in the current context, one may have a good number of people attracted to these special events for whom connection with the church community is not important. They may find themselves attracted to a church event primarily because they like Bingo, Trivia Night or a Holiday Fair, for example, and attendance at church sponsored activities is their only real connection with the church. One would most likely not find them attending the church's services of worship or programs in religious education. In my view, this does not make a case for eliminating these kinds of events but what it does is pose these questions: *How can the local church best demonstrate the heart of what Christianity is about, i.e., how can the church find ways to center activities around the concept of outreach to others, known in Christian terminology as discipleship? How can the church communicate its mission to those who touch base with it because of the appeal of the social activities it offers?*

Ultimately, the lure of Christianity is intended to be the teachings of Jesus and the practical implications of that message for our lives. Consequently, in this era wherein church attendance has declined and there is little that draws many people of good will to churches, it makes sense both religiously and practically for churches to center themselves on expanding opportunities to serve others, with the motivation to follow Jesus their primary guide.

In my view, this movement toward perceiving and presenting the local church as a community of disciples rather than a social club can go a long way toward providing not only the sense of belonging that has long marked church communities but also the wider sense of purpose or mission as used in much of church language. Implicit in this understanding is that *just as Jesus was a person for others, He was someone for whom reaching out to those in need or alienated was central to His life, so too should the church seek to be outwardly directed.* While this is not to say that a church should not pay attention to its own organizational needs, it *is* to affirm that the church's primary focus has to be centered on what was the primary focus of Jesus, as described so directly and powerfully in the words of Matthew 25:31–46, a passage to which we will keep returning and which is important that we have in front of us as we continue our reading:!

How do we make this happen?

It all begins with the concept of sending:

In the service found in the worship materials used by the Evangelical Lutheran Church in America (ELCA), we see the structure of the typical worship Sunday worship experience. This is a structure that has formed the core of much of Christian worship through hundreds of years. This four-part structure provides for the flow of the service. Understanding this structure is integral to an understanding of both worship and practice, as well as the significant relationship between the two.

   a. *Gathering*—The process of the service begins with people coming into the worship area from both near and far. They come from the world in which they have lived since the last time they gathered in this building or place designated for worship. In a sense, this gathering process really begins in one's own home! The very decision to attend worship is in itself part of this gathering activity.

   b. *Word*—As they engage themselves in this worship time, they can listen to and reflect upon some of the texts that constitute their religious tradition. They hear passages from the Bible and focus on the Gospel which conveys to them a message from the life and teachings of Jesus A preacher then proceeds to speak about something she/he views as integral to the readings of the day in relationship to the living out of one's daily life.

   c. They share in the *Meal* that calls to mind the night before Jesus died. This meal, of course, is shared within the broader context that those gathered believe that they are doing so within the framework of faith that Jesus, though once crucified, remains alive in this moment and always, and is somehow present in their midst. In fact, he is present in the word, the meal and in the very gathering of each other! What really struck me as quite powerful when I first began exploring

Church: Social Club or Community of Disciples?

Lutheranism and the writings of Martin Luther was this explanation of Holy Communion, as found in Luther's *Small Catechism*:

"What is the benefit of such eating and drinking? The words "given for you" and "shed for you for the forgiveness of sin" show us that forgiveness of sin, life, and salvation are given to us in the sacrament through these words, because where there is forgiveness of sin, there is also life and salvation. How can bodily eating and drinking do such a great thing? Eating and drinking certainly do not do it, but rather the words that are recorded: "given for you" and "shed for you for the forgiveness of sin." These words, when accompanied by the physical eating and drinking, are the essential thing in the sacrament, and whoever believes these very words has what they declare and state, namely, "forgiveness of sin." Who, then, receives this sacrament worthily? Fasting and bodily preparation are in fact a fine external discipline, but a person who has faith in these words, "given for you" and "shed for you for the forgiveness of sin," is worthy and well prepared. However, a person who does not believe these words or doubts them is unworthy and unprepared, because the words "for you" require truly believing hearts." [1]

d. *Sending*—At the conclusion of this time of sharing word and meal, those present are now sent forth to go back into the world where this very cycle starts once again. *They are sent forth to live out the values that have been expressed and prioritized throughout the worship experience. It is extremely important that this act of worship not be perceived as separate from the tasks of daily life!*

Ideally, this cycle continues week in and week out, with the culminating part of the service being the sending of the congregation which is charged with living out its faith through all the ups and downs of daily life!

While in some denominations, the inclusion of the *meal* does not take place on a weekly basis but may be reserved for once a month or unique occasions, the essence of this structure is expressive of the experience of worship to be found in the community of people known as church. With or without the celebration of Communion, which is my ordinary preference, with room for variations and exceptions, the experience of worship is centered on the influence that Jesus has upon this group of people gathered.

1. Luther's Small Catechism as printed in *Evangelical Christian Worship*, the worship book of the ELCA.

This influence of Jesus can be found in the stories about him that are told (Gospels) as well as the Biblical readings that come to us from the tradition in which He was raised (Judaism) and the attempts to piece His life together with the daily lives of those who would be His followers. These are articulated in the variety of letters as well as other significant writings found in what we have come to call our Bible's New Testament.

What I am saying here is that at its core, the experience of worship provides us the opportunity to focus on the heart of the Christian message and to give us the impetus to seek to live that message in our everyday world. This is quite contrary to a rules emphasis found in the religious understanding of many which is centered on an obligational mindset. In this context, attendance at worship is really part of the cycle of Christian life, i.e., it is a way to connect both with the core teachings at the heart of Christianity and with the people who are committed to living out these teachings in the ways that shape their everyday lives.

OUR PERCEPTION OF WHO WE ARE AS A CHURCH

While when we gather as church, it is good and healthy that we connect with people with whom we feel comfortable and enjoy being around, what is of primary importance in how we perceive what it means to be church is found in this: *It is important that we see ourselves more as a community of disciples and less as a social club.*

First, we must be clear: There is nothing wrong with people in a church enjoying the simple experience of being together. This communitarian aspect of church has been present since its inception and is extremely important. However, it is crucial that local gatherings of people who identify as churches have an understanding of themselves as disciples of Jesus, i.e., as centered on the teachings of Jesus.

Given the fact that people affiliate with churches for a variety of reasons, there is some complexity in this. To understand this complexity, it is helpful to examine why people opt to affiliate with a church. Among the plethora of possibilities, these appear to stand out:

- Long standing family affiliation
- Experiences one has had in college, military and other 'away from home' situations

- A personal crisis one has gone through or an experience of great personal joy
- The example one has found in others in one's workplace, circle of friends, etc.
- The influence of someone with whom the individual has formed a close relationship as well as how this notion of faith may have become relevant as expressed in the relationship itself.

Consequently, in purely practical terms, it does not necessarily follow that because one has affiliated with a church, he or she has had a profound religious experience which has moved one in that direction. There are too many other potential factors involved. Nonetheless, given the relatively small percentage of people who relate to and connect with a church community and attend services frequently, one might be able to assume that, due to the voluntary nature of such affiliation, a good number of people for whom church is part of their lives have found themselves motivated by a fascination with and perhaps an allegiance to the teachings of Jesus of Nazareth.

As a result, it makes great sense to focus one's self- understanding regarding the importance of church in one's life on the significance one places in seeking to live out the teachings of Jesus and the self-awareness one has that she/he is in some sense called to discipleship, following the life, example and teachings of this man, Jesus of Nazareth. Under that general umbrella may very well be found a variety of doctrinal and practical differences. This manifests itself in the variations one finds in denominational affiliations, for sure. Nevertheless, the core focus on Jesus and one's attempt to, in a real sense, follow Him provides a good explanation for the importance of the role of church in one's life as well as for the practical actions a church might be expected to carry out, including the consistent and ongoing practices of service to others (all others) and to the act of peacemaking as reflected in the life of Jesus!

THE IMPORTANCE OF REAL-LIFE EXAMPLES

For the experience of church as community of disciples to be real, participants need to draw from the inspiration of real-life examples of Christian faith in action. These examples are present in different places. They may very well include fellow members and friends of the local church community whose lives are incredible examples of positive inspiration. I could go on and on about the examples I have known in the churches of which I have been a part. For as long as I shall live, I will always remember the examples of people such as these:

- The chaplain at the college I attended who inspired me to see the deep connection between the Gospel of Jesus and the pursuit of peace and social justice. He was heavily involved in protesting our presence in Vietnam and supporting efforts to bring an end to that conflict. In his ministry as chaplain, he brought many speakers to our campus who spoke on issues of justice and peace. Among others, these included Jane Fonda and her then husband Tom Hayden, well known and controversial activists opposed to our nation's approach to war.

- The quiet service of people, one, whom I knew at the Catholic church I served as a deacon, who, behind the scenes and with no fanfare, went out of his way to be sure that the needs of struggling folks in the community were met [2]. I saw the same spirit evident in many people, one, in the first church I ever served as pastor, as well as in other places I have served since that time. While I really could go one and on about those whom I have known in my life who set such great, inspirational example, I have another point to make as well.

In looking back at my life experience, I have found myself reflecting on how important it was that at varied times in my own faith development, I also found myself inspired by those who were more well-known public figures, i.e., individuals whose action drew the attention of others as examples of putting one's Christian faith into practice.

What is interesting is that along the way I have also learned that most of these people were also individuals who were quite controversial, even to the point of making others angry at them. In my view, these were people who really stood out. They were individuals who incarnated in real life so many of the things I had learned through my years of religious education.

All too often, what we are taught in the world of religious education is a lot of dogma and doctrine. I do not deny its importance. However, doctrine and dogma can be rather stale and flat and might even seem irrelevant when

---

2. This man, John Nachyly, was one of the kindest I have ever known. He was deeply engaged in coordinating the efforts of the St. Vincent de Paul Society and did much to help those in need in the community in which he lived.

compared with real life example of what it means to live out one's life as a sincere, serious follower of Jesus.

Over time, I discovered many of these inspirational examples. As I have mentioned, some were people I knew who were not in the public spotlight but were good people committed to serving others and to affirming the dignity and worth of other human beings.

However, I would also wish to add that I have likewise found great inspiration in those whom we might call public examples of a Christian life well lived. In my years as a teacher and preacher, I have sought to talk and teach about certain inspirational individuals such as the ones I will describe below. I have found that telling stories about real life exemplars of discipleship made real and concrete serves as a source of inspiration to others as I am convinced that, way down deep, the human person seeks to find meaning, purpose and deep conviction in the arena of one's life.

It is important in offering these real-life human examples to note that there are many others whom I have known who, in ways unknown to a wide population, live out the Gospel values of Jesus. As the old hymn goes:

"They live not only in ages past. There are hundreds of thousands still. The world is filled with the glorious saints who long to do Jesus' will."[3]

So, as a matter of principle, as a preacher and a teacher, I have encouraged people to read and learn about those in the Christian tradition whose lives were exemplary in that they took the core of Jesus' teachings and put them into practice. Among those whom I have preached and taught about over the years; these have stood out to me:

DOROTHY DAY

Founder of the Catholic Worker movement, Dorothy Day is an incredible living example of someone who did not simply talk about outreach to the poor, but who lived it! As of this writing, the Catholic Church is considering the possibility of canonizing Dorothy Day as a saint.

---

3. From the hymn ' I Sing a Song of the Saints of God'

DIETRICH BONHOEFFER

A young German Lutheran pastor who, in standing up to the Third Reich in the heart of World War Two was executed by firing squad at the young age of 36.

CESAR CHAVEZ

Here was a man who supported the rights and needs of farm workers who were deprived of fair wages and humane working conditions. His lettuce and grape boycotts, all done in the spirit of nonviolence based on his faith in Jesus, ultimately led to better living working conditions for those for whom he spoke up. I was thrilled to hear him speak in person when I was a student in graduate school in Boston. As a result of his example and his passion, I went years without eating a single grape, a fruit I happened to like a whole lot. In addition, every Saturday for a couple of my collegiate years, I would get up early in the morning and go to the grocery store at the foot of my college's hill and proceed to hand out pamphlets encouraging consumers to boycott both lettuce and grapes because of the horrific mistreatment of farm workers which I had learned about from this man. On a personal note: I think it is wonderful that America's President at the time I am writing this has a bust of Cesar Chavez positioned in a prominent place right behind the seat at his desk in the Oval Office. Years later, as a religion teacher in a Catholic school, I showed a film about the work of the United Farm Workers and the pain and anguish the farm workers endured. This was incorporated into our school's social justice day, which I coordinated.

JEANNE DONOVAN

A suburban Connecticut woman with academic training in business who felt an inner need to go to El Salvador and serve the children living under a cruel, oppressive regime. Her change in lifestyle led to her assassination at the hands of government forces.

OSCAR ROMERO

A traditional, conservative Catholic bishop in El Salvador who found in the plight of his people the inspiration to consider what the Gospel was all about. Archbishop Romero was assassinated at the altar while celebrating Mass because of his public criticism of the immoral practices of the Salvadoran government. I highly recommend that, if possible, you take the opportunity to see the film simply entitled *Romero*.

DANIEL BERRIGAN AND PHILIP BERRIGAN

Daniel was a Jesuit priest who with his brother Philip, also a priest and a graduate of Holy Cross, my own alma mater, stood up against the forces of violence that led to America's involvement in some highly questionable wars. Not only was I able to read a good deal of Father Daniel's work but I was also able to spend time listening to him and his brother at public presentations on college campuses during my collegiate years. These in person experiences were incredible in so many ways and have left a lasting impression!

There are many more examples that I could give. Yet, I bring up these names and encourage you to explore other ones to make a simple point:

It is important for those in the local institutional church to be fed with examples of Christianity in practice. It is not enough for individuals to perceive their church as a place *to go to worship* without, at the same time, seeing the real-life implications of what we learn through the process of worshiping. By concentrating on learning about lives which are shaped by putting the words of Jesus into practice, we can see more fully what Christian faith and the purpose of the church is about. *While what we may call doctrine or dogma is important, the core of Christian faith is in the impact one's beliefs might have upon one's actions.* In citing examples of those who lived out their faith so profoundly, we can grasp the depth of this enterprise and thus able to see the church as being in practice what is described in its language-the body of Christ in the world.

PRACTICAL WAYS OF DOING DISCIPLESHIP

This all leads into my contention that local churches need to seek out means of living out a discipleship which engages congregants in an ongoing outward focus. It strikes me that people who are part of a church community really need to see the connection between what they profess and how those beliefs have impact on the real world. I would suggest that churches have a focus on *local needs and options for serving those in their community. This, however, requires, some explanation.*

There is a danger in a local focus. The danger is that people can all too readily ignore the reality that Christian outreach is intended to be directed not only at the people down the street from the church but also those in other countries and parts of one's own nation. *A local only approach can, at times, be just too easy and limited.* However, the fact remains that congregations which exist in local communities are most likely surrounded by people nearby who need help. These are individuals who might need food, shelter, or access to important medical or psychological services. While there is a danger, a spiritual danger, in clinging to a *take care of your own approach*, it is important that even when reaching out to those outside of one's community that one not ignore the issues right around the corner. *It is a delicate, yet necessary balance.*

Over the course of time, many churches have, perhaps unwittingly, taken on the *take care of your own* approach to social outreach. To be clear, it is important that we as individuals, civic groups and religious bodies are attentive to the needs of those who live near us. It *is* important to take care of our own-in our family, our neighborhood, our church, our city, town or state! *However, if we do not watch ourselves and limit our interest in social needs only to those around us, we are falling short of embracing the full teachings of Jesus, whose own personal outreach included actions directed at helping those outside of his religious and ethnic community, as well as those within it.* I would also suggest that we consider expanding the notion of who, in fact, really constitutes our own. I would suggest that Christian faith would affirm that *'our own' is comprised of everyone!*

My point in all of this is fourfold:

1. Outreach to those in need is integral to the work of the local church.

2. Local churches must be selective so that they are able to both identify *and* prioritize local needs.

3. Churches should be active in helping to meet the needs of the communities in which they reside and function.

4. However, at the same time, the local church has a responsibility to be attentive to the needs of God's world outside of the local domain as well. In looking back at experiences I have had in churches of which I have been a member, prior to entering the process of pursuing ordination, I think of the local Catholic parish to which my wife and

Church: Social Club or Community of Disciples?

I belonged in the early years of our marriage. This church had an incredible, deeply rooted commitment to the needs of the people of Haiti[4] and aligned their efforts with those of a Connecticut diocese to raise peoples' awareness of the abject poverty found not far off the shores of the United States. This raising of consciousness evolved because of the commitment of dedicated individuals in that local church and has a definite ripple effect! Maintaining a universal awareness is extremely important to the ministry of the church, even as it remains attentive to real human needs in its own backyard. It is a delicate, yet necessary, balance!

PUTTING THIS INTO PRACTICE

There are really two key activities related to this issue that local churches need to consider:

1. *Someone in church leadership in addition to the pastor must be identified who has a passion for recognizing needs not only locally, but beyond the parameters of the church's geography.*
2. *Once identified, these needs should find their way into action.*

I wish to cite two examples from churches I have served:

When the tragic Flint, Michigan water crisis struck several years ago, an event occurring halfway across the country from the setting of the church I was serving as pastor, our church's youth led the process of bringing in an outstanding singer[5] who incorporated music about social justice, concern for others and world peace into her performances. While we as a church paid out of our budget to have her come, the proceeds from her performance taken up in a free will offering went directly to a church of our denomination in Flint and to their direct outreach to those in need of help in dealing with this crisis. We did not charge money for people to attend the concert, but we advertised a free will offering targeted at the people of Flint and we engaged in communication with the local church coordinating the outreach in the Flint community.

In another situation at four different churches where I have been pastor, we have brought in an outstanding speaker from the organization

---

4. St. Bridget Church, Manchester Connecticut
5. Kristen Graves. See www.kristengraves.com

Simply Smiles[6]. He spoke at worship regarding the plight of Native Americans on reservations in South Dakota and in Mexico and the active support given them by his organization. In two of those churches, we ended up doing a concert for the benefit of this incredible organization. At a small church I once served in Connecticut's smallest town, the passion the young people had for this important cause was a catalyst leading to raising a good deal of money for its important work.

To do these events, one of the most important elements involves identifying these real-life human issues beyond our native towns and the locations where these churches functioned. In these and other outreach concert and presentation situations with which I have been involved in local churches I have served, these events, without detracting from ongoing local outreach, have served as an effective means to communicate the needs of a broader world than we would see if only looking locally!

There are several other examples I could give of ways to assist a church to be much more than a social club and center its sense of self on an understanding of what it means to serve others as disciples of Jesus who, after all, is the reason we have such a reality as that which we call church!

---

6. Bryan Nurnberger, its President and Founder

5

THE CRISIS OF CHURCH DOCUMENTS

LET ME BEGIN BY SAYING that I would not be terribly surprised were you to look at the title of this chapter and say something like *"Yeah, the crisis of church documents . . . so what?"* I am going to assume that most people when thinking about church are not thinking about so called church documents, much less with what may be contained within them that may constitute a crisis. As a result, this could easily seem like an irrelevant and rather boring chapter!

However, before you skim through this chapter quickly or rush forward to Chapter Six, I wish to suggest that you consider this: One of the positives to be found in American Protestantism has been that, in the way church governance and management is structured and in the language of the local church's most important document, that of its Constitution and By Laws, what we will find consistently is a focus on the active role of members of the church who are *not ordained* in the ongoing process of making decisions within the church.

Consequently, were one to read these documents, one would find that the leadership and hands on management of the church's finances and the actual decision-making power in terms of spending money and making consequential decisions about church matters is in the hands of the laity of the church, i.e., people who are not ordained pastors or in other ordained ministries within their denomination.

Now, of course, there are nuances and distinctions between and among different churches within the Protestant tradition. Nonetheless, the contrast with the Roman Catholic polity with respect to the role of lay persons is obvious and most significant. This is something I experienced firsthand throughout my years of service in the Roman Catholic Church, including my years prior to ordination when I served on the elected parish council, the typical Catholic term for what is known to many in Protestant circles as the church council.

The clearest contrast in these approaches is found in something quite basic: *In the Roman Catholic model, ultimate decision-making authority on the local level is in the hands of the parish priest who is the church's pastor.* While he must answer to the bishop and while his decisions cannot trump the bishop's own, *he* does hold a considerable amount of final decision-making capacity within his local parish (congregation).

What emerged within Protestant church communities from the time of the Reformation moving forward was a more collegial model than anything found in Catholicism. This included the active investment of non-ordained persons in broader decision-making situations and roles within the congregation. In fairness, despite their theological emphasis on the priesthood of all, many Protestant traditions did continue the practice of placing its pastor on a pedestal, even as its theology was focused in a different direction. However, Protestant theology that emerged from the Reformation most clearly leans in the direction of a shared priesthood of all believers.

Nonetheless, it is important to note that the reason for this more collegial model found within its documents centers on this basic fact: Many of the earliest established Christian churches in the United States, particularly in New England, were those of a congregational background in terms of what is known as church polity. They were often established as part of the center of local towns and quite often dating back to the early years in the life of that town. Their polity emphasized the role of the congregation in making important decisions about the church. The pastor alone would not be the decision maker!

In New England, for example, these churches would meet for worship in the same meeting house in which local town meetings were conducted. Many clergy, who in Roman Catholic tradition were appointed by bishops, were chosen in Protestant churches through a process of being called to service by the congregation itself. To structure this well within the church, local congregations established constitutions and by laws which were based

The Crisis of Church Documents

on the structure of the governing documents found in local towns in which these churches were established.

In other words, the governing documents of churches within the Catholic and Protestant traditions stood in direct contrast to one another. In fact, within Catholicism, except in rare cases, parish councils really never came into existence until the period of the Second Vatican Council in the early 1960's.

Now, perhaps you are asking: "*OK, where are we going with all of this?* "If you are sympathetic to the Protestant governing style or polity, you might very well be inclined to think of this as a good thing. I get that and I agree to a great extent as well. However, I would also like to posit that the presence of these church documents also carries with it something of a dilemma, a dilemma best explained this way:

A lot of emphasis in Protestant church councils has focused on something of a separation of duties between clergy and laity. In its most extreme form, it can be explained as simply as this: The lay people take care of the finances and the building, and the pastor takes care of the spiritual stuff!

Let's break this down a bit:

One could say that it is fair to see how this makes sense. To be a pastor, at least in a mainline church, one must go through considerable academic training involving in depth exploration of the Bible, church history and the history and theological focus of one's denomination, along with many other things. A pastor must be trained in providing counseling and spiritual direction as well. For many pastors, ordained church service is her/his sole profession.

The expectations for a church council member are different. Perhaps he or she is a businessperson, attorney, teacher, farmer, doctor, insurance agent, engineer, banker, dentist, factory worker or part of any number of other professions. Whatever job or profession that might be, the person's primary academic training and/or life experience is not in the same areas as those who prepare themselves for a career as a pastor. Consequently, a tendency often creeps into the local church evidenced by a church council which focuses on money and building issues with the pastor, on the other hand, concentrating on the spiritual.

As a result, what can happen, be it clearly or covertly, is that councils and their leaders can quite easily focus on their primary role as that of handling the money and the building. Now, of course, to repeat: This is important! However, in the process, unless a council works at it, it can easily slide away from a very key role that it needs to play, a role that is built into its ministry as part of the *priesthood of all* that is so important a concept within the Protestant context.

Church documents, e.g., constitutions, by laws and the like, thus become a crisis when they inspire people to separate the roles of pastor and congregant to an unfortunate and extreme level. In more practical terms, churches need lay persons to engage in processes of growth and reflection on the spiritual issues that underlie the decisions they will need to make.

Unwittingly, it would be quite easy for lay council members to see certain aspects of church ministry as being simply the pastor's domain when their background in the non-clerical world can in and of itself be a phenomenal resource within the work of their church. As a side note, there *is a* flip side to this as oftentimes, the pastor is expected to have knowledge of a lot of the technical stuff regarding the functions within the building to the point where some members might lose sight of the fact that this is not intended to be her/his primary focus as she/he exercises pastoral leadership within the congregation. Many times, over the years when I have served as a pastor, I have been asked specific technical questions regarding the lights, electrical circuits, sound system, boiler or other equipment within the church building. Knowledge of such things is most *certainly not* my area of strength. I know that there are pastors far more skilled in this than I am. I also know that, throughout my years as a pastor, there have been many, many members of the congregation who were knowledgeable and well skilled in these areas. A pastor with technical background can be a great asset to a church. However, it is not essential that she/he have that background. What is ideal, however, is that some folks in the congregation might!

Since church documents read so much like those found in town charters and by laws, it makes considerable sense for people to see their roles involved in taking their skills and helping the church through their use of them. The fact that a businesswoman, for example, who has a strong financial background, can be a great asset on the council of a church is a wonderful thing. *However, that same businessperson is a Christian, striving to live her life as part of a church that both feeds her spirituality and serves as a community which affirms the teachings of Jesus. In reflecting upon her role as a council member, it is important that she look at herself in terms of what she must bring to the life of the church. This, of course, includes the unique gifts she possesses because of her professional role and her observations of what the church needs to do to live out the mission of Jesus.*

That *Jesus focus* must be a common task in which all lay leaders of churches need to engage, alongside the engagement of their ordained pastors.

'ALL MEANS ALL'—REFLECTING ON THE 'PRIESTHOOD OF BELIEVERS'

In the ideal world, one which, quite frankly, I think, is not at all pie in the sky but, in fact, quite doable, it would be a wonderful thing if people who were freely connected to the community called church approached their commitment by assessing honestly how through this connection, they are able to both nourish their spiritual lives and, at the same time, contribute to the living out of the church's purposes and mission.

All of this, of course, raises the question: What are the purposes of the church? It is a *very* important question!

The church is an institution. Most churches have buildings in which they worship. The upkeep of buildings costs money which explains why some churches, reflecting on what it means to be church, have raised questions regarding whether we need to look at the building issue differently from how we have in the church's past. Many lifelong church members would be troubled by the implication of what I just stated. For them, their church building evokes important emotional sentiments- They were baptized, confirmed, or married there, their parents' funeral was there, and they want theirs to be as well . . . They sat in that same pew for years and that experience provided a kind of spiritual comfort . . .

For all these reasons, the maintenance of these buildings taps into something within many folks which connotes a connection of spirit, in a very real way.

Yet, looking at this from another perspective, some others would think about church and react a bit differently. Some might say that even if the same people were gathered in a different place that looked nothing like the one they have known all of these years, that even if the stained-glass windows they loved or the cross behind the altar were no longer there, this would really be their church because of the connections between and among the people who were. Some might even raise questions as to whether the church is fulfilling its mission inadequately by pouring so much money into buildings instead of zoning in on the core teachings of Jesus as described in Matthew 25!

One must also note that, with some exceptions, it is quite possible that younger adults and teenagers may not, in general, have as much connection to memories attached to a building as those of generations prior to theirs. As I state this, I do so with some caution because in my experience as an educator, I have seen 20-year-old college juniors come back to their old high school and react negatively to some of the physical changes they have seen there, claiming that it just does not feel the same as it did when they were in high school only a few years back. I suppose that no generation is exempt from at least some degree of nostalgia. I would also suggest the probability that most high school graduates would have a stronger connection with their schools than they had with any church.

So, having said that, when it comes to church issues, given the high percentage of youth who, in their childhood and adolescence, *did not* have a strong connection with the institutional church, it would seem that the nostalgic yearnings for the old worship space would not be quite as intense as mine were when I drove by the old motherhouse of those nuns for whom I served Mass, a motherhouse now converted into a privately corporate run prep school, a chapel no longer containing that element of sacred space that I had last experienced over 40 years prior to making this drive at the age of 68!

WHICH BRINGS US BACK TO THIS . . .

The focus of this chapter has been on the matter of church documents and how what's contained therein can also be a source of crisis within a church. Within a year or so of serving in one congregation and observing the process of going through council meetings, I concluded that it was time to do a workshop for council centered on going through the church's constitution and bylaws. I happened to decide that I was going to try to do this several months into the COVID-19 crisis which relegated all our council meetings to the world of cyberspace, in particular *Zoom*[1], a great tool which, unfortunately, tends to work better on some computers than it does on others.

My goal in offering this workshop was twofold:

---

1. An online site which became quite popular as COVID 19 struck our nation and the world.

1. I felt it important to look at our current practices and how they align with the theology that undergirds them. I thought that exploring some theology would help convey the message that this document is about much more than a bunch of parliamentary rules and procedures, not at all unlike what you might find at a local school's parent advisory group or perhaps the local Kiwanis or Rotary club.

2. I thought it would be a great way to get people thinking theologically. A good example was how our bylaws provided for an Evangelism Committee. It struck me that it was important to help people reflect theologically at what evangelism might mean and how one puts that into practice, practically speaking. In my experience over the years, I have found that the word evangelism has often become synonymous with strategies for getting new members and that the intent and depth of the very word evangelism has been lost in the process!

To be honest, the response to that session ranged at best from indifference to someone's serious question put to me challenging why we were taking up time having this conversation. While some of these reactions reinforced my position that we really *do* need to look at how our practices align with what we have put in writing, I also realized that, even though I had spent a lot of hours readying myself for this session, I had not prepared as well as I should have.

In retrospect, I should have asked more questions. At that time, I was a relatively new pastor there and I should have delved more into the history of how the structure with which the Council identified these tasks, e.g. Evangelism Committee, evolved. I should have gone more biblical and theological and led a discussion more focused on the meaning of and the misuse of the term evangelism.

Side note: It is important that I reiterate what I have said above: My experience in churches is that evangelism, a term connected with sharing the Gospel, has become a code word for providing church activities that are going to yield more numbers of people attending that church. Evangelical efforts tend to include, depending upon the church, bingo nights (can I help my Catholic upbringing?), church suppers, movie nights, church picnics and other events in keeping with the perceived interests of those coordinating these evangelistic efforts.

I Love the Church, I Hate the Church

I AM STILL CONVINCED . . .

Though I do not give myself terribly good marks, a C- at best, I would say, for the way I approached these matters at that Zoom meeting, I will say something positive as well. I am still convinced that the intention I had behind this was good and a necessary one indeed. My purpose, in a nutshell, was to get people to reflect on the meaning behind some of the language we use in churches. In this case, it would have meant digging deeper into what constitutes *evangelism* and proceeding to see how we can best shape evangelistic efforts within this church community. I should have explained more about how I think the depth and meaning of the word *evangelism* has not been developed fully within local churches who use the term. Perhaps I should have scrapped the idea of centering a meeting on an entire church document and limited our exploration to the very meaning of the much-used word *evangelism*. That may have very well led us into a serious conversation about what we can do in terms of community building or facilitating the process of the church feeling like an open, inviting and welcoming community of people- individuals who may very well enjoy having the opportunities to share a meal, go bowling, play softball, enjoy bingo, trivia night or movies, while at the same time recognizing that the church exists to live out the teachings of Jesus, as expressed in the gospels and the lived historical experience of the worldwide community of faith that goes by the name of church!

I would also add that, upon reflection, what struck me in this situation is something I have seen in many churches. *What I am referring to is the tendency not to spend enough time exploring the theological meaning behind those things that churches do.* Were one to take the word *evangelism,* for example, interpretations would vary from the evangelism espoused by many conservative churches to an understanding of evangelism that I saw in my own mainline church, i.e. somehow connected to activities which would bring people into the church and would promote the proclamation of the gospel of Jesus within the context of the neighborhood and community in which the church resides.

Overall, through this experience, I learned that those charged with leadership positions in a church have the responsibility to both learn about and teach the meaning behind the documents that shape their structuring. By doing so, these statements become far more than a bunch of words in a constitution many might find 'too boring to read' and rather provide a foundation to shape a vibrant, active church community, where defined terms contain a lot of real life, practical meaning. I have learned as well that what is contained in these documents needs to be explored, updated, and presented as important, even if some of the language within them and the interpretations that have developed over time need to be updated and renewed!

In the ideal sphere, these documents fall desperately short of what they should be if they do not inspire people to do some serious thinking and to move beyond the words contained within them into a way of being church which is both practical and spiritually inspirational! Those entrusted with these documents have an obligation to read them, discuss them and apply them to the realities of what it really means to be the church!

6

We Have Always Done It that Way

In the year 2002, thirteen years after my ordination to the Roman Catholic permanent diaconate I was ordained a pastor in the denomination of a Protestant church, the United Church of Christ. In that same year, I began an eleven-and-a-half-year period of serving a church that had been founded in 1738. Most recently, I served a church congregation that was established in 1957 and in between I have worked in churches both old and comparatively young. One dominant phrase any pastor can expect to hear at some point usually early in her/his tenure at that church is a simple, direct, and potentially powerful one, usually expressive of at least a subtle kind of criticism. What's the phrase that is on my mind and is making its way to the pages of this book? I will bet that you have all heard it somewhere along the way- in your family, at work, or maybe even in your church! The phrase? It is easy to remember: *"We have always done it that way"*.

The fact is that churches are institutions which, much like all institutions (Rotary Club, Elks, Knights of Columbus, and so on . . .) rely *on traditions*. Over a period of time, those connected to those institutions, including the local church, have become accustomed to and expect certain events to take place and certain set ways of doing things to occur throughout a calendar year, with events that are important in marking time in the institution's life. Somewhere along the line, a way of doing certain things first occurred and then eventually took hold within the local church. This could include anything from the special events the church sponsors to the way that worship is conducted.

We Have Always Done It that Way

It is important to note that on the psychological level, there is a value and a purpose to these traditions and to the consistencies to be found within them. In some cases, such as the example I gave of the Circle of Fun event in my home Catholic parish back in the day, they help to mark a certain season and stand out to us as all part of the circle of living out our lives. As I comment upon the *"We have always done it that way"* phenomenon which is part of church life, it would be easy for the reader to be zoned in on the apparent criticisms I am making of events and practices that are of great importance to those who engage in them and look forward to the season coming around when those will be part of the life of the local church. I can cite as example the fact that the coming of the Circle of Fun at St. Mary's Catholic Church in Putnam signified to us children and our families that the school year was fully underway and that it was our common task to support this school and the parish that made it all possible and had done so for many generations! This was much the same way as the local Woodstock Fair on Labor Day weekend reminded us that summer was over and it was time to go back to school!

My intention here is not to be critical of those events or practices that shape and give meaning to our lives. Looking back at my own childhood and teen years living at home, there were several events both in church and in the community that I, along with many others among my peers, looked forward to with great anticipation. In the world outside of the church, there was the local Fair that took place (and still does) each Labor Day weekend. In the life of my Catholic parish, there was that annual Fall event on the church grounds which I have referred to several times as well as the church dinners, Communion breakfasts and raffles that were part of the church's annual calendar .As an altar boy for a national headquarters of Catholic sisters, also known as nuns, I looked forward to serving at the annual Corpus Christi procession, a festive occasion made even better by the great food I would have the opportunity to eat for free as part of that celebration. One town over from where I lived, as a student at Marianapolis Prep, a Catholic secondary school, I worked at an annual Lithuanian Catholic event that took place in the summer, a fun filled celebration with great food and enjoyable activities, all supporting and affirming the traditions of this strong Catholic ethnic community, a community responsible for the very foundation of my school!

These events and the many more that are part of church life depending on the history and ethnic backgrounds of each individual church community helped those of us involved in them in so many ways. They provided something we could look forward to each year, opportunities for social interaction, good food and fun as well as a feeling of connection to something greater than ourselves. In addition, they broke the pattern of what we might call ordinary time. In a life filled with daily work or the tasks of going to school, these events offered something to which we could anticipate as activities that would both break the monotony of daily life as well as provide unique opportunities for connecting with others.

During this extended period of staying at home because of the COVID-19 pandemic, I had the opportunity to catch up on a program that aired in my house every Saturday evening over 20 years ago, *Dr. Quinn Medicine Woman*. Though it was on TV every Saturday night, its two viewers in our home were my wife and then young daughter. During much of the year, my sons and I were downstairs watching sports. Between being Red Sox fans as well as supporters of UCONN basketball during some of their glory years, we always found something good on TV each Saturday evening.

However, I had been told by both my wife and daughter about how wonderful a program *Dr. Quinn* was and it was not until pandemic time that I had the opportunity to sit down and appreciate it by watching a great number of its episodes. One of the many things that struck me about this program which highlighted life on the American frontier and the tensions between Native Americans and those who took control of the land was the importance of different events within the life of those who lived in these little towns and who spent so much time working so hard. I was struck by the rituals provided by each of these special community events, which often included fun, games, food, and music, all taking people away from the monotony and the anguish of an extremely busy work week both at home and on the job.

It is quite clear to me that for the people in my little town, myself included, these church sponsored events I describe provided the kind of respite I saw in that television program. While the conditions in 1960's Northeastern Connecticut were different from those in frontier days, an awful lot of people I knew, moms and dads of kids with whom I went to school and played Little League baseball, found in many activities sponsored by local churches opportunities to unwind, connect with others and simply have a good time in the midst of a life in which their weeks were so often spent working exceptionally hard. The activities of the church provided opportunities for that kind of respite, often spoken of theologically as periods of Sabbath rest.

We Have Always Done It that Way

THE NEED TO ASK QUESTIONS

To respond to the needs of both the church community and that beyond its walls, of first importance is the willingness to ask good questions. First and foremost, among those questions is a very basic and direct one: *In crafting activities and programming within this church, what are we trying to accomplish?*

There could be many answers to this question, including the omnipresent *"raise money."* While it is important for churches to be solvent and take in the appropriate amount of funds to carry out its work, *a singular focus on raising funds is highly problematic.* In my view, the structuring of church activities does best when focusing on two primary areas of focus:

- *Serving the needs of people both within the congregation and in the community beyond it*
- *Sustaining the financial functioning of the church*

In terms of preference and fidelity to the church's mission, the logical priority would be that of service.

Nonetheless, I have learned in my years serving churches that one cannot simply dismiss the importance of paying attention to finances also. Paying attention to and being focused on and unyielding about financial expenditures are two different realities. While I will fully, freely, and gladly admit to being a liberal, *I will also say that my definition or description of liberalism does not include wanton, wasteful expenditures of money in a church's budget.* In my view, the process of developing a budget is one that focuses on serious conversations regarding church priorities, all based ultimately on the underlying values of the church community. *As I see it, this always goes back to the teachings of Jesus and how to apply them within the church.*

I would ask that those who, like me, would identify yourself as liberal or progressive not tune me out at this point! What I would like to do is share with you how and why I approach this question of finances the way that I do:

In my view, when one is constructing a budget that focuses on meeting real human needs, it is important that money in that budget not be wasted on extraneous items. As you know from reading my biographical description, I was an employee in my state's public school system for thirty years. I would be the first to claim that many of the school budgets that passed within the system where I worked for thirty years included all kinds of unnecessary items as well as an unwise approach undergirding them.

Let me start with this example: Let's suppose that a particular department in a school has a budget of $5,000 for supplies. *For purely hypothetical purpose of example,* let's say it is the Social Studies Department. Let's also say that four weeks before the end of the school year, the department head and faculty realize that they have only spent $2,500 on the budget. It seems to me that this fact would indicate the lack of need. In other words, there was no clear-cut perceived need to spend money on items that were not important.

Sad to say, in situations such as these, I have seen departments take this approach: They have sought to find things to spend the unused money upon so that they would be sure to use up the money and maybe get more appropriated to them in the next budget year. As I see it, this is not reasonable stewardship of funding. The purpose of a department budget is to provide for what students and teachers in the department need. This might include books, videos, money to bring in guest speakers, money to send teachers to worthwhile conferences and the like. If departments work intelligently at ferreting out unnecessary expenditures, teachers and students alike could benefit from the good experiences that will come from the money expended. In fact, as one who gladly self identifies as a liberal, I have long seen this kind of exorbitant, unnecessary spending as one of the most illiberal actions possible. My reason is that when people perceive wasteful spending, they are disinclined to spend money for those items or positions that are truly needed.

Now, how might this apply to a church? Well, I have seen firsthand how money built into the budget to pay for a variety of church items has, within its own context, been a waste of money at the time at which it was spent. The reality is that certain times call for measures one would not use at other times. A good example of this is found in what churches have experienced in the experience of dealing with COVID-19. With less income coming directly to church communities and typical rental fees for building use being nonexistent because the building is not being used, money budgeted for certain expenditures that are nonessential could easily become wasteful spending as well!

Now, please do not get me wrong: Do not read my call for fiscal common sense to, at the same time, be a plea to cut spending for programs that impact people in need. To the contrary, I favor increased spending by churches on programs related to social outreach! In fact, I believe that what can give a church room to spend more on outreach that meets real life human needs is the process of cutting back on wasteful, unnecessary expenditures!

A hypothetical example:

Let's say that the youth group of a church comes up with the idea that they could draw a lot of young people in the community and its surroundings to a concert sponsored by their church by a local well-known musician whose music leans in the direction of promoting social justice, human rights, economic equality and direct outreach to the hungry and the poor. Let's also recognize that since making music is this person's way of making a living, these young people are faced with having to pay $ 1500 for this person to do a two-hour concert in the church. (As you may have already figured out, this is a real-life situation, described in a previous chapter).

Let's also say that at the time the annual budget was constructed, this concert was not on the radar but now is a different matter as the issues of concern to this musician have just so happened to have bubbled to the top of peoples' social concerns. Consequently, there was no budget line which would allow for $ 1,500 to be spent on a concert!

Now, apart from the fact that my preference is that churches float out possible expenditure policies in structuring budgets, given the reality that the church has budgeted no money, how can they reasonably make provisions to offer a free concert with free will offerings going to the worthwhile cause they are espousing?

Realistically speaking, to make this happen responsibly, they would have to make decisions to withhold spending from other budgeted items. For example, what if the pastor has not used up his/her $ 600 line item for continuing education? Perhaps he or she does not really need those magazines or books or continuing education conference on this topic at this time. In prepandemic years, that might include foregoing one's plans to have the church pay for a $500 flight to some conference for pastors somewhere, as well as food expenses while there. Maybe some of that, along with money used in other church endeavors, need not be spent right now.

Ideally, of course, the best solution to this on an ongoing basis is built in budgeting to allow for the funding of programs/events that were not even known at the time of the construction of the budget. Taking $ 100 out of the cost of books or travel to a conference could help to create a fund that might contain a sum of over $ 1000, for example, which could be targeted under the general category of special events, i.e., those events that were not on the radar at the time the budget was created.

What I am advocating for here is that churches need to have the flexibility to respond to changing and unforeseen circumstances. Ideally, the recognition that these circumstances could appear on the radar is a good starting point! In the ideal world, it would make sense for churches to consider annual budgeting with this reality in mind . . . even if they have never thought of doing it that way!

And . . . sometimes things just happen . . . . . .

Before I was ordained a clergyperson in a Protestant denomination, I had accepted a position of director of Christian education at a local congregation of the United Church of Christ. It had seemed clear during my interview that members of the congregation on that search committee were really interested in what I expressed as a strong commitment to youth ministry and to engaging teenagers in the life of the church, one of my foremost interests throughout the years I had served in different local churches. Consequently, they offered me the position and I embraced it completely!

Soon I began to learn more and more about the impact of something I knew about when I took the job. This church was in deep pain and reeling from the allegations of misconduct of their well-respected former pastor, a man held in high esteem by members of the congregation of all ages, including those adolescents who were part of the Confirmation program which I was charged with running, many of whom were deeply affected by the turmoil that had developed in their church.

To make a long story short, I was fortunate enough to develop a good relationship with the young people and their parents. Likewise, I was fortunate as well to serve with two women who were simply outstanding clergypersons.[1] Much of what I learned from them would influence me when I became an ordained pastor myself, ordained in that very church building where I was most privileged to serve.

Through my conversations with our youth and with many of the adults I had been able to get to know quite well, I discovered that within our body of young people we had some with remarkable musical talent as well as a strong penchant for acting. I concluded that, based on what I had gotten to know about these young people, the climate was just right for a youth production of a musical that would be inspired by the teachings of

---

1. Rev. Susan Prichard and Rev. Cynthia Carr, First Congregational Church, Vernon, Connecticut

We Have Always Done It that Way

Jesus. I had a particular production in mind as I engaged in conversations with our youth about potential options.

That musical that struck me as just right was Stephen Schwartz' exciting production *Godspell*, based on the life and teachings of Jesus and containing a really wonderful, multi layered soundtrack. We also happened to have, among our youth, a young man who would go on to great success in music and who would nearly twenty years later end up being the church musician at the church I have most recently served[2].

It was clear to me that if we could get the support of the church council and proceed to go forward with this production, we would get a great turnout and we could contribute positively to the emergence of a positive feeling among our youth and within the wider congregation.

However, there was a slight problem. *The youth budget I had inherited had a grand total of two dollars left in its account.* It would cost about $1500 simply to pay for the rights to produce this musical. With the pastor's support, two of the youth, including the musician whom I have mentioned previously, came along with me and made a case to the church council asking if it would be possible to garner their financial support. Now, having gone through the recent crisis of losing a pastor under troubling circumstances, let's just say the church was not swimming in money so freely that it could turn over the amount we needed.

Despite this, the youth who spoke to our council made a very convincing case that we would all work very hard to get a lot of people to come and that we would encourage folks to be generous during the time when a 'free will offering' would be taken up.

So . . . here was the situation:

The youth budget could not pay for the rights to this musical so the proposal on the table was basically to roll the dice , so to speak, and hope that a good number of people would attend our suggested three performances and that they would collectively put enough money in the collection plates we would pass around or buy some ad space in the program that we would be printing that we could at least break even. The contention we who supported this project made was that this kind of experience would be both good for the church and profoundly meaningful to those who would be involved in it, especially considering the difficult circumstances with which this church had been dealing.

---

2. Eric Hutchinson, currently serving as church musician at Grace Lutheran Church, ELCA, in Plainville, Connecticut.

I Love the Church, I Hate the Church

Amazingly, the council decided it was worth this financial risk. The result was truly incredible All three performances packed the house. As a result of the voluntary offering we took up as well as the sponsorship from many members of the congregation and others, we brought in an amazing amount of money, well above what was needed for the cost of the production. This money could be channeled into worthwhile youth activities going forward . . . . .and it most definitely was!

This experience was one of the greatest I have had in all my years of working in churches. On the day I was ordained in that building years later my mind was filled with memories from that *Godspell* weekend. That production started a tradition of youth musicals in that church and the young man so deeply involved in coordinating the music went on to direct productions of *Jesus Christ Superstar, East of Eden,* and, along with another exceptionally talented young man, co-wrote an original musical entitled *Believer*, all of which filled the capacity of that building in subsequent years. And went on tour in different venues in New England.

Apart from my memory of my then 10-year-old son volunteering to collect money on opening night and coming to me astonished when someone had thrown a $ 100 bill into the basket he was passing around, I have this powerful recollection from our third and final performance. It was on a Sunday afternoon and we were most fortunate that we had received many reservations for youth groups from a variety of different churches to attend.

The director of this play, a good friend of mine with whom I worked in a school for 11 years[3],and I took a little down time prior to the start of the production and on this beautiful Sunday afternoon, hung out outside of the front doors before we would go back and get to work inside. So, as we stood there watching as people got out of their vehicles when time for the start of the show drew near, we saw a van pull in from a Methodist church and a huge number of young people come out and head in the direction of the entrance to this play.

Not long thereafter, I said" *Look at this Joe*" as I watched in amazement as youth walked down the street of our church, coming over the hill from their local Episcopal church. Before long, a large group of Unitarian young people came in their van and took their seats alongside adolescents and their leaders from churches in the United Church of Christ, as well as Lutheran. Catholic and other UCC congregations.

The result of all of this was fivefold:

3. Timothy Edwards Middle School, South Windsor, Connecticut

1. A church community that had been reeling in pain found enthusiasm and hope.
2. Youth from our church connected with those from other congregations.
3. Older folks drew inspiration from young people and youth enjoyed their affirmations and their conversations with them.
4. The message of the Gospel, the core of the message of this play, was conveyed in an original, nontraditional way, using an approach that could speak to the human spirit, even should that spirit have no previous connection to or interest in Christianity or if they had long since given up on the institutional church!
5. While all things had been done in ways that had not been attempted in that congregation before, because they were done so faithfully and convincingly by those who directed the play or who acted in or supported it, this effort produced something new and energetic that marked this congregation as alive, well and attentive to the spiritual needs of all, including our youth!

SOME SUMMARY OBSERVATIONS

Every organization and institution is susceptible to *the "We have always done things this way"*mindset. This phrase or sentiments reflective of it pop up in churches in varied ways. One classic example centers around some questions involving worship.

One of the most helpful experiences for me in my work as a pastor of a church has been the experience of serving as a supply pastor in those times in my life where I have been in between calls to settled pastor positions. When one serves as a supply pastor at a church she/he may never have been in, one needs to learn the procedures and protocols of how worship is celebrated there, in that building.

Each church, over time, has formulated ways of celebrating worship which may very well vary from the ways worship is done in other churches. Some of this occurs because the church and its pastor have really kept up with reading and discussing documents on worship or attending workshops. Some occurs because though changes have been made throughout the broader church, those changes have not found their way to this local one. It is not unusual for pastors to be very comfortable with what they have established as their typical way of officiating at a worship service. *I am sure that I have been susceptible to this over the years, even as I try not to be!* Sometimes, it occurs simply because the fact is that there really is *no* one way to do a particular liturgical action. For example, over the course of my career, I have officiated at Eucharist services using different prayers and points of emphasis at the table.

I have found that there are people who attend worship regularly who can get really thrown off by the fact that the person leading worship sometimes (or often) veers away from the *way things are always done*. While I would never advocate for change for the sake of change, I would contend that there are a wide variety of ways to worship and an exposure to this variety is a good thing for all!

ONE FINAL NOTE . . .

Nearly 40 years ago, I began studying for a degree in counseling. I was most fortunate to have had many outstanding professors, many of whom were trained therapists in practice themselves. I was sitting in class one day listening to a fascinating lecture by one of them when I was struck by the insights he shared with us. He told us that on this day, we were going to talk about what people need to make them feel comfortable, especially when it comes to group settings. His insights have long struck me as profoundly applicable to many aspects of life and I quite readily would apply them to my experience of church!

My professor told us that we all as human beings have a need for:

Affection: That which comes from feeling accepted and deemed as worthwhile.

Inclusion: This is connected to affection as it is that would make us feel that we are a PART of the larger experience, that of the group, which is now happening

Control: As individuals and in a group setting, we all need to feel that we have not only a stake in what is happening, but also the capacity to influence it, that is, to have some degree of control within it.

This analysis of the inner dynamics of individual behavior within groups explains a great deal. In the context of the church, this is how I see it:

While one is part of a church because of what is ultimately an individual's own decision at some point, at any time, if her/his participation, regardless of the person's age, that experience of church is to be meaningful, needs to be one in which the person feels included and through which the individual both receives from and gives to others the sense that they are an integral part of this community. Likewise, the person, to retain identification with this group, must have a sense that she/he has control over some of the decisions made within that group.

It appears to me that it is possible for people to be troubled by those changes that veer away from the *way we have always done things* because those changes have shaken something contained within these three needs described and defined above! As a result of this insight, I would then suggest that congregations and church leaders do whatever they can to work together with these basic needs in mind. When these needs are respected and nurtured, it is so much easier for people to venture out and to try something that they have never done before, finding in that experience an exposure to a certain depth within the religious experience of church that simply was never there, until they took that leap!

In practical terms related to what happens in churches, I offer an observation I have made from, as I said prior, quite a few experiences of visiting a church as a supply pastor, somewhat akin to a substitute teacher, I would suspect:

Over time, each local church has developed its own protocols and procedures for worship. This includes ways of setting up the altar, doing Communion, putting the order of service in its bulletin (or up on a screen) and many more . . .

The key issue in all of this centers around whether there is more than one way to do certain actions in worship. I strongly believe that there is. That can include a variety of prayer formats and of actual actions in worship. It might include sometimes being more 'formal', other times more informal. It most definitely includes an understanding that there is more than one way to celebrate Communion and that there is more in the worship book than might meet the eye of those who are used to one style of worship all the time. I mention this in reflecting upon a church I know who had a long-term pastor and whose style of worship never really changed over a period of several decades, a period in which the institutional church as we have known it was undergoing significant disruption and chaos.

I will conclude this chapter with an example and a comment:

One day I led worship at a church where I was not the pastor and prior to worship met with the deacons who would be sharing in leading Communion. One wonderful individual explained to me in great, specific detail how Communion would be done in this church's worship service. He noted that after I finished speaking the words of institution, I would then take the elements off the table and would give them to the deacons who would proceed to share them with the congregation.

I encourage you to think about this and the explanation I gave him:

I told him that what I was going to do instead is to ask him and the other deacon to take the bread and wine (grape juice) right off the table themselves and then proceed to distribute it to the congregation. Now . . . I get it if you, the reader, would say I am being picky here, but I want to explain my point:

I told this deacon that I do not want the liturgical action to convey the impression that there is a hierarchical order at Jesus' table. To distribute communion, the deacon need not receive the tray as if it were coming down to him hierarchically from the ordained clergyperson. Instead, I contended, the ones distributing the elements share in the function of serving at the Lord's table, including, in this ritual, the simple act of presenting the plate from which the bread or drink may be received.

Though many of us may have been part of churches where *things were always done this way*, it is important to be in touch with the whys of these traditional practices and wherever the tradition gets in the way of conveying the best possible meaning of the action, veering from tradition thoughtfully and kindly, can be a very good and often necessary thing!

As is so wonderfully expressed in the worship books within the Lutheran tradition, specifically the ELCA, there are four basic movements at worship where Communion is shared: We gather, we hear the word, we share the meal and alas we are sent to go into the world and live out that cycle again. Within that framework, there is flexibility and when we say that we have always done things in a certain, intractable way, we may very well be missing out on something that could nourish our spiritual lives, as well as that of the wider congregation!

7

THE CHURCH AS COUNTERCULTURAL

I FREELY CONCEDE TWO things within which context I suggest you consider this chapter: First, my formative years were in the 1960's and secondly, I am a huge fan of Bob Dylan. You may wonder why I would begin this chapter by stating these two facts. Well, the response I would give is this: Without a doubt, many of my views about institutions and traditions have been shaped in a period, the 1960's and early 1970's (which for all intents and purposes were really still the 60's)where change was in the air, a time when raising questions and challenging assumptions had actually become quite normative for people in my generation.

WHICH BRINGS US TO BOB DYLAN . . . .

In reviewing the great songs that influenced the culture in which I grew up, Rolling Stone magazine cites Dylan's *"Like a Rolling Stone"*[1] as being on the top of that list. As I see it, there was something in that song that spoke to what was happening within American society. Even beyond that, these words, coupled with its accompanying riveting music, touched many people of my generation and were expressive of conflicts emerging within us. This powerful piece of artistic work came on the heels of Dylan's assertive declaration just a few years prior which served to remind a culture that

---

1. A popular song written and sung by Bob Dylan.

"*The Times Are A Changin*" [2] and that our society and world were living in the midst of that whirlwind of change in the present moment.

WHICH BRINGS US BACK TO THE CHURCH

A long time ago, as a college student in the early 1970's, I was required to read a book by H. Richard Niebuhr for one of my courses which is entitled *Christ and Culture*[3]. In fact, as part of the requirements in one of my courses, I was also expected to know it quite well, at least well enough, that is, to participate somewhat intelligently, in our class discussions about it! The book contains an amazing amount of both significant insights and information, for sure.

At that point in my life, for some reason, I was struck by the clarity of the material in this book. For me, it placed a focus on the *different ways* Christian faith interacts with the broader cultures in which we all live. As I have grown older and spent a lot of years participating in the life of several Christian church communities and holding some leadership positions in several of them, I have found myself coming back to this book for insights and for consideration. The core conviction expressed by Niebuhr in this classic work is that there are five potential ways in which faith in Jesus Christ has an impact upon how we relate to the broader culture in which we live. Niebuhr identified these ways as follows:

1. *Christ Against Culture*
2. *Christ of Culture*
3. *Christ Above Culture*
4. *Christ and Culture in Paradox*
5. *Christ as transformer of Culture*

What does this all mean? In essence, I found these exceptionally helpful in identifying the various ways in which the church impacts the culture in which it exists. For example, there are some who would see Jesus as entirely antithetical to the culture in which people seek to live out His teachings. For some, this would mean identifying Christ's church as being above and beyond the culture in which it resides.

---

2. Also, one of Dylan's most popular songs.
3. *Christ and Culture, H. Richard Niebuhr*

This, of course, is in opposition to the notion of Christ as belonging to that culture. Carried to its extreme, this could lead one to see the values of a nation and the teachings of the Gospel as eerily similar. Another position focuses on a Jesus who is above culture, more engaged in the spiritual realm and less immersed in the things of earth, an intriguing position stressing the paradoxes, i.e., apparent contradictions between that which is of the Gospel and that which represents the values of the culture.

Yet, it is the last category that I find the most intriguing. In fact, I would contend that it is this perspective on the life and teachings of Jesus that has the best available practical merit.

In looking to Christ as transformer of culture, we acknowledge that there are things present both in Jesus' teaching and the way that He lived out His life that provide a legitimate challenge to the values that may be found within the culture in which we exist.

As an example of how this view might function, we can return to the Sermon on the Mount in which Jesus encourages praying for those who persecute, turning the other cheek, not returning evil for evil and so on.

Taking this a step further, it also seems fair to raise the question: How does the church stand in relationship to these teachings of Jesus? Does the church's focus carry out the mission espoused by Jesus in the Sermon on the Mount and the Beatitudes as well as the powerful message presented in Matthew 25:31–46, a message connected to the Last Judgment?

CONSIDER THIS:

If we are to see Jesus as, in fact, *inspiring* the church to be a change agent within the broader culture, what exactly are the implications of that? As we have said earlier, we are looking at the distinction between the church as social club and the church as a community of disciples. What I am saying here is that what Niebuhr identifies as the Christian faith in relationship to the broader culture most assuredly applies to the church in relationship to the wider world, including yet not limited to the local community in which it exists.

SOME SAD STORIES:

Bear with me a bit as I take you through a few of the things I have seen in my years as a pastor. As I see it, reflecting over the years, these anecdotes speak powerfully of the need within church communities for focusing deliberately and regularly about the ways in which we present ourselves. Noted below are some experiences I have had in various churches I have served over the years. I write them without referring to the church in which they took place and with the recognition that the behavior pointed out here represented a general pattern that is not in the sole possession of any local church alone. So, with that in mind . . . here goes . . .

- I am hanging around church on a given Sunday morning about 30 minutes before the service began when one of the church leaders, a very dedicated man who cared deeply about the church, came running into my office to tell me that someone had just come in off the street and was sitting in one of our pews. This man also noted that this individual was unkempt and could have used a good bath or shower. This regular church goer was very concerned about this person's presence.

- A church member comes up to me after worship to express her concern about some new person who has started showing up at worship and what she perceived as some of this woman's bizarre behavior at worship. This behavior included her propensity to ask a lot of questions of the pastor.

- Another person expresses concern to me that someone who appeared to be under the influence of alcohol had just showed up at the church.

Beyond these specific anecdotes, over these twenty plus years I have worked as the pastor of a church, I have had people, usually church regulars who would engage me in conversation about new people who just happened to show up at Sunday worship who somehow seemed different. Once, several years into serving a church, after I had finished commenting on how wonderful it was that we were getting a good number of new people in attendance at worship, the person with whom I was speaking responded by downplaying what I thought was a terrific thing and pointing out that we really can't expect much money to come in from these new people. There were all kinds of implications in that statement, wouldn't you say?

The Church as Countercultural

ALL ARE WELCOME

The hymn *All Are Welcome*[4] has been a favorite of mine since the moment I first heard it decades ago. In the first church that I served as pastor, I introduced that hymn early on and it became a reference point for how we sought to present ourselves as a church. In fact, it was that hymn and the implications attached to it that I wrote about in my doctoral dissertation entitled: *Preaching and the development of church identity in a small town.*

WHEN I CAME BACK FROM CHICAGO . . . ..

During one of my summers studying for my doctorate in Chicago, it became clear to me that many churches were taking concrete steps to insure that people were aware of the church's openness to same sex marriage as well as to insuring that all people, regardless of sexual orientation, felt welcome within the institutional church. I was committed to sharing with my congregation the need to have an extensive opportunity to explore the issue by providing opportunities for study and discussion. Consequently, I offered a four-part educational series in which I presented varied theological perspectives regarding the issue of homosexuality and the church. While I personally favored the rights of homosexuals within church communities, including same sex marriage, I structured my educational series much as I had structured classes when I taught religion in Catholic high schools. My method involved presenting both sides of the issue objectively with particular attention to insuring that people could understand the reasons which led people to espouse a particular point of view. While I did mention that I was going to propose a change in favor of allowing marriages for homosexual couples to occur within our church's sanctuary, I encouraged people participating in these sessions to pay careful attention to the *why* behind each side's point of view, even to the point of being able to articulate it, even if it were antithetical to their own position! To this day, I am so proud that this little church in a rather conservative small Connecticut town, amended its constitution and bylaws to allow for the pastor to perform same sex weddings within the sanctuary of that church. They did this at a period before the nation turned more favorably than ever in the direction of marriage equality for all!

---

4. This hymn, written by the distinguished composer Marty Haugen, has found its way into the hymn books of Catholic and Protestant churches.

I was also quite fortunate in this small-town church which I really loved dearly that we had an amazingly vibrant and committed Youth Group. Our overnight retreats in our church building would draw as many as 25 young people in a town of barely 700 residents overall at that time.

OUTDOORS BEFORE WORSHIP: OUTSIDE OF THE BOX

I really liked the Youth Group we had developed at that wonderful little church. These kids were open minded, creative, and deeply caring! As this sense of the importance of *welcoming* as integral to a church's life was a characteristic embraced by these youth, I asked several of them to help me really put this into concrete terms one Sunday morning at worship. I have no problem saying that it was a rather unorthodox way to start off a typical Sunday service!

So, what I did was come up with a plan where when people showed up for worship, as they entered the front door and walked by the lawn, they would notice that there was movement and noise coming from someone lying underneath a pile of blankets. That person so happened to be me, but the folks coming to worship did not know that! The young people were in on this project and assured the rather stunned members of the congregation who walked by that all was under control. From what I heard, there were several adults who were wondering if the police should be called and all of that, but they determined that this was not necessary because the person under the blankets appeared to be non-threatening.

Well, a few minutes later, after the congregants had been seated and the musician's prelude began, it was time to sing the opening hymn. As the organ began playing, this person covered with blankets and unknown to those sitting in the pews took a processional walk up the aisle in this small, intimate sanctuary. This was all happening as the congregation was singing (or supposed to be singing . . . they were rather shocked!) the hymn *All Are Welcome*. This individual proceeded to go up behind the pulpit and then take the blankets off, thus revealing himself as none other than the pastor of that church . . . Me!!!! Obviously, this approach to the beginning of a worship service could be considered outside of the box. However, as I planned it, I became more and more convinced that it was quite appropriate in a catechetical sense, i.e. as a way of teaching some core values integral to

The Church as Countercultural

Christianity. *In addition, my years of teaching have taught me that to make a point, it is important to get very, very concrete.*

In this case, I knew the point that I wanted to make. I was looking to raise the question of what it really means to be *welcoming*. The situation of showing up for a religious service on a Sunday morning and finding something going on one's church's lawn which is less than ordinary carries with it the capacity to force one to look at what it means for us as individuals to welcome others . . . and to mean it! It might challenge us with questions: Are we OK with welcoming if we are only welcoming those of our own kind?

This unusual event led us into a message which raised these kinds of questions and provided material for us to consider how we as this little church in a small town could be that kind of community. It really sparked a lot of reflection, as well as a good amount of discussion. In fact, it was so far outside of the box that it's the kind of thing many of these youth told me they remembered this in conversations they had with me many years later! Another outcome was that I did not get fired for doing this, which indicated to me how open this congregation was to the concept that *ALL* are welcome.

Most pastors will tell you that they have experienced what I am about to describe: One comes into a church on a given Sunday morning and unlocks the doors only to discover that not that long thereafter someone has entered who has not been part of this church before. In some cases, that someone is ill kempt, not dressed in typical Sunday church clothes. In other situations, it might be obvious that the person is hung over or under the influence of drugs. In one church I served, it would not have been unusual for one of these guests to have spent a night in a shelter. At times, people have just dropped into churches I have served with a lot on their minds. I have had individuals ask me for reading material about God. I have had others ask me outright to lend them some money.

In the churches in which I have worked as pastor, the clothes they were wearing and their manner of presenting themselves were not in keeping with the ordinary dress code of that congregation, even though I never served a congregation that had one in writing. *Thank goodness!!!*

Over time, the presence of those whom I would call seekers, i.e., people who are longing for a life better than what they have been experiencing in the life they are currently living, has posed a good, healthy challenge both to me as pastor as well as to the congregations I have served. The challenge it has presented is that we, the established members of a Christian congregation, must take seriously the words we use. *If we say all are welcome, we need to mean what we say.*

In a culture and in a world which has a history of bias, prejudice, segregation, and all kinds of ways of emphasizing that people should 'stick to their own kind' even within the church, this is the challenge to run counter to the norms of the culture and, most importantly, to really embrace the values of Jesus of Nazareth.

When the church is willing to act in ways one might call counter-cultural, the community of faith not only opens the doors to individuals seeking meaning and purpose in their lives! It does so much more! In these actions, the church serves as a community of faith which, through their actions- of acceptance, welcoming, outreach and empathetic listening, as well as concrete giving as needed (be it giving clothes or providing information about social services individuals may need), the church is functioning as a force which is profoundly countercultural, much in keeping with its founder and inspiration, Jesus of Nazareth, *the one who annoyed people by reaching out to the marginalized and disenfranchised, those who somehow did not fit the norms of the social or religious culture in His own time!*

8

Do We Need the Church?

THE INSPIRATION FOR THIS CHAPTER comes from a book by the same title, written by the late Richard McBrien, a renowned Roman Catholic theologian whom I was most fortunate to have as a professor in graduate school. In his writing, McBrien highlights the belief that the community called church and its institutional component should no longer be seen as the center of God's plan for salvation. Instead, the church is to be seen as both sign and instrument of the reign of God, in traditional language known as 'the kingdom of God.' McBrien focuses on the belief that while *all are called to the Kingdom(reign), not all are called to the church*.[1]

This is an important distinction! As I see it, it posits the *reign of God* as accessible to people and cultures of a wide variety of religious persuasions. In McBrien's view (and mine), the life and teachings of Jesus are expressive of what the reign of God is all about. The community known as church is one in which people seek to be disciples of the man Jesus, whom we acknowledge as one who formed a community of disciples (followers) who would go by the name church. One of the most important points that needs to be made in the preaching and teaching of Christianity to all generations is the importance of defining and experiencing church as community, as opposed to viewing it as an institution instead. I oftentimes point out to people in both my preaching and my teaching that we must be cautious about using terms such as " I am going to church this Sunday."

---

1. From book noted above

This is not a simple matter of nitpicking! My point in emphasizing this is that, in reality, those who seek to follow Jesus are the church! We may happen to worship in a building that has been given the name church but in essence, *the church is the people, not the building.* This, of course, was a central highlighted point of the Roman Catholic Second Vatican Council which described and defined church as the people of God. In my teaching and preaching to congregations I have served, I sought to phrase this more in terms of emphasizing the idea that *"We are the church who gather together for worship."* I really try to avoid any language that gives the impression that the church is a building. It is important, in my view, to emphasize that the church is *people, described in the language of Vatican II as the "people of God."* Somewhere during my educational and theological background, I learned that words really matter. In retrospect, I think I must give the credit to the high school English teacher who had a great impact upon my educational life! [2]

As is obvious and is common knowledge, attendance at worship has shown a precipitous decline in most mainline Christian churches over these past few decades. Sunday mornings (and Saturday evenings for those in the Roman Catholic tradition) are quite different these days from what they were not that many decades ago. The church parking lots most crowded are not the ones which surround what we have described as the mainline Christian churches. The high probability is that a church with a filled parking lot is most likely to be one out of the evangelical wing of Christianity. Of course, this word evangelical has sadly been linked to conservative Christianity, far removed from its original intent!

These trends have been quite troubling to those for whom church attendance and participation have been very important over the years. It is necessary, I think, to take some time to consider why church attendance and participation had been important. When exploring this, we come face to face with different reasons:

- For some, attendance at worship has been a law, i.e., a rule or regulation of a particular Christian church. With respect to this, Roman Catholicism offers the clearest example. In traditional Catholic theology, there is an obligation to attend Mass on Sunday and on specific holy days of obligation. While it remains a law within the Catholic tradition, the reality is that, in current practice, most baptized Catholics

2. Mr. Guy DiNocenza, my English teacher for three years at Marianapolis Preparatory School in Thompson, Connecticut.

are ignoring it as indicated in the decline of attendance in Catholic churches and the accompanying church closures over these last few decades.

- For most Protestants, while the *legal* obligation to attend worship has not been part of their tradition, the *value* of it has been paramount. Consequently, were one to look back to decades such as the 1950's and at least the early 60's, one would find a much higher percentage of people in Protestant churches attending worship or Sunday School back then than what one would find today. I have spent a lot of time looking over church directories for the churches I have served, and it is amazing to read the statistics concerning church attendance in different decades. Likewise, it is quite informative to look at the pictures that show crowded Sunday schools and packed pews on Sunday mornings. In one church I have served, when I first started doing my research as I started my ministry there, I found an 80% rate of attrition in terms of church attendance and affiliation with the church that had taken place in one recent decade alone. That was a very significant indicator of many different issues and a reality I could not ignore as I moved into the early days of my pastorate there!.

While people in both Catholic and Protestant traditions as well as those within Orthodox communities have bemoaned the decline in attendance, what lies beneath the actual statistics are some very important questions: What is so important about attendance at worship? What is or should be its appeal? What would be the incentive to attend worship? While I will be addressing these questions in the paragraphs to follow, I want to go a step further and ask an even deeper question. I would like to cut to the heart of the matter and put this one on the table: *Do we need the church? Of course, this poses another question: When you say the word church what do you mean?*

Starting backwards, I would pose a simple definition of church. *I would state that, at core, the church is a community of human beings who seek to follow the example and teachings of Jesus and to apply those to their lives.* I would then break it down a bit by saying that the word community is a key word in this description. In connecting with other human beings who share the same convictions about Jesus, there is a commonality and a sense of cooperation in what the church does. People, for example, might join with other church participants to help serve the needy or advocate for causes. They might even seek to raise money so that varied ministries of the church might flourish.

As the reason for the church has to do with the belief that Jesus makes present to us the reality and, we might say, values of God, the church's task is to:

- Tell the stories of Jesus
- Experience the meal he shared with His dearest friends as He faced impending death
- Put into practice the values embodied in both the stories *and* the meal. *We do this through the lives we lead both inside and outside of the church building!*

Now, none of this is as simple as it might look when put down so succinctly on paper.

Let's explore why:

"Jesus left that place and went away to the district of Tyre and Sidon. Just then a Canaanite woman from that region came out and started shouting, "Have mercy on me, Lord, Son of David; my daughter is tormented by a demon." But he did not answer her at all. And his disciples came and urged him, saying, "Send her away, for she keeps shouting after us." He answered, "I was sent only to the lost sheep of the house of Israel." But she came and knelt before him, saying, "Lord, help me." He answered, "It is not fair to take the children's food and throw it to the dogs." She said, "Yes, Lord, yet even the dogs eat the crumbs that fall from their masters' table." Then Jesus answered her, "Woman, great is your faith! Let it be done for you as you wish." And her daughter was healed instantly."[3]

In other words, when a church tells the stories of Jesus, what is important is that there be people in the church who have a good handle on how the Bible developed and who are not susceptible to the dangers inherent in fundamentalism. Were one to look at this passage at face value, one could readily:

1. Be irritated, angry, and confused with the way in which Jesus treated the woman in the story.
2. Be somewhat thrown off by the simple fact that Jesus changed His mind. For some believers, that very action would pose a challenge to

---

3. Matthew 15:21–28

their position that since Jesus is God, God is not going to act in any way that might be considered questionable ethical behavior! Consequently, interpreting this passage poses a number o challenges!

It would seem obvious, of course, that a church's pastor should both have an extensive training in how what we call the Bible developed and some of the debates that exist among Bible scholars. It would also be ideal if people within the congregation who do not do professional church ministry for a living take interest in the background of the Bible. This could be through quality adult education within their congregation or through some more developed study on their own.[4]

3. This knowledge of scripture should carry over to how people come to understand the sharing of Communion. At core, those who are part of the church need to understand the link between the sharing of Communion, usually within the church's sanctuary, and the living out of the meaning of Communion in the life of the broader world!

All of this brings us back to the key question of this chapter: Do we need the church?

My own answer response to my own question would be in the affirmative: Yes, I believe that we do!! However, in answering this question with a yes, it is important for me to explain what I mean when I say this:

I am not saying that we need the church exactly the way it is externally. With absolute due respect to the traditions in many churches, I would nevertheless contend that for the church to be the church, it does not need huge cathedrals or basilicas, nor clergy donning expensive garments. Please do *not* misunderstand me . . . One could make a case that in certain historical contexts, the way a church building was constructed made a powerful statement and affirmation of Christian faith. For example, in a culture that was dominated by white Anglo Saxon Protestants, where there was clear discrimination against Catholics and immigrants in general, the building of churches on a hill, buildings that would stand out and be noticeable, often from great distances, made a powerful statement to those who saw them. They made the statement that Catholicism had arrived here, right in the heart of the city or town, present as a means of proclaiming faith in the

---

4. As a starting point, I would highly recommend that people consider taking the time and using the materials accessible at www.enterthebible.org, a resource from Luther Seminary in St. Paul, Minnesota.

crucified and risen Jesus! However, one might contend that this position is not necessary today. In examining this, I want to resort back to my experience when I was in college:

Every day at 5:30 pm as I alluded to toward the beginning of this book, students at my school, an institution run by the Roman Catholic Society of Jesus, popularly known as the Jesuits, offered a worship opportunity to members of the student body, faculty and others who worked on the campus. People would voluntarily gather in the lower Chapel to participate in what is popularly known in Catholic parlance as the Mass. *This is also known as the celebration of the Eucharist.* Those of us who grew up Catholic and had our share of experiences of going to Mass discovered something here in this college setting that was very different from that which we knew growing up and attending and perhaps serving as altar boys in the typical churches and chapels where the Mass was offered daily.

Here are some of the differences:

- In the typical church setting, the altar, i.e., the table upon which the elements of bread and wine were set was 'up front' and the participants were in pews and looking upward at the altar from their vertical location. However, in this worship setting, a different one from my previous experiences, we were all seated up front near and around the altar (table) with that table in the middle. Now, this all made complete sense to me, even though I had never experienced it, because it got me thinking that if we are calling to mind Jesus' Last Supper when we gather for what we call Eucharist, Communion or Mass, what did Jesus do at the Last Supper? He sat at table, surrounded by his closest friends.

- In the churches I attended and served as an altar boy as a child and adolescent, there was a routine in which the same specific prayers were said regularly. In this new setting, while the structure remained the same, i.e., we listened to Bible readings, we confessed our imperfections, we shared Communion, we offered one another the sign of peace, we prayed for specific intentions, how we did these things was significantly different. The language of the liturgy was often complemented by spontaneous prayer or prayers from different sources connected to the theme of that day's worship or of the events taking place in the world as we gathered that day for worship.

- In praying for specific intentions, people felt comfortable speaking personally. Room was provided for people to personalize. The prayers of intercession, also known as" prayers of the faithful" within Catholic liturgical parlance, provided room for specific personal intentions to be shared in language often far less structured than what would find in the usual liturgical texts.

- In preaching the sermon (homily), it was common for the priest presiding to sit in the middle of the circle or speak from the table and quite often, this presider/preacher would engage us the participants in this liturgy, in sharing some of our own reflections spontaneously or in asking questions.

- Communion was shared not by forming a line and coming forward from the pews but rather by passing the elements, including the cup of wine, around the circle.

These regular experiences of worship had an impact upon me. In Catholic parlance, they pretty much left an indelible mark upon my soul. I came to discover that these Eucharistic experiences were not limited to that chapel. The years when I attended college were ones in which significant changes were happening within the worship practices of the Catholic Church. In the area where I attended college, home Masses took on a certain popularity among segments of the Catholic population, often presided over by Catholic priests who had chosen to marry, often including messages (homilies) delivered by women, a practice that was not normative in the typical Catholic parish. There was an excitement to this liturgical renewal in varied pockets of Catholicism that would affect me as I moved into my future as one who would be charged with presiding over worship in Protestant churches.

It is important to be clear: In saying yes to the question *"Do We Need the Church?"* I am not saying that it is only through affiliation with a Christian church or only by affirming oneself as a Christian, can one reach eternal salvation. If the question is: "Do individuals have to be Christians to attain the joys of heaven?" I cannot in good conscience answer that with a yes! What I am saying though is this: What we call the church is at core a community of people who freely and willingly affirm that the life and teachings of Jesus are intended to have an impact upon the broader society. In effect, the conviction of those who take this position is that it is Jesus' view of life that provides for those who pay attention to it some core principles as to how one should live out one's earthly life.

I Love the Church, I Hate the Church

With respect to the above statement, one needs to ask the question: *How* does the church do this? My response is that it does through several different ways:

Paying careful attention, first and foremost, to understanding what Jesus taught and how He put those teachings into practice. There are some specific ways that we can do this. It involves holding up Jesus as a role model and seeking to imitate His values and actions within the context of one's own life. It also involves an understanding that the church is a community of those who share these principles and intentions. Likewise, it places priorities on holding to the recognition that the community of people called church exist to have influence on the broader, wider world. *A starting point for this centers on recognizing that the principles the church community holds can intersect with principles held by communities of people of varied religious persuasions or none at all.*

I would contend that that this understanding of the nature and mission of the church is one which is consistent with the teachings and convictions of Jesus of Nazareth and provides a way of unifying those of good will who hold religious convictions yet are open to finding in each other points of agreement and deep-seated conviction! To this point, I wish to cite some examples:

- It is possible for someone to claim he or she is an atheist or agnostic but finds the concept that the human person should see value in all human persons and treat humanity with great respect. This is a conviction that could very well be shared with those who hold to religious beliefs as part of an organized institution. However, it is one that would not necessarily require that sort of dogmatic conviction to be operative. The work of Karl Rahner is exceedingly helpful here, particularly a careful reading of his term "anonymous Christian." The writings of Fathers Jim Bacik and Harvey Egan, both scholars whose work has centered on Rahner's theology, is quite helpful and I recommend it highly![5]

- Likewise, it is possible that one who is a believer and espouses a religious affiliation outside of Christianity (ex: Buddhism, Judaism, Islam) might find significant points of connection between her/his beliefs

---

5. As a starting point, I would recommend accessing their work via the Internet, as much of their material is posted there. It is a good starting point!

Do We Need the Church?

and those found among people who look to Jesus as the moral teacher who provides the basis for their convictions. We see this in Mahatma Gandhi's affirmation of Jesus' Sermon on the Mount as moral teaching worth emulating, as well as in the positive comments about Jesus, especially regarding his ethical teachings, espoused by those who take issue with many of the convictions of the institutional church regarding Him and who struggle with much established Christian religious doctrine. A good example would very well be Thomas Jefferson[6].

The overriding question we asked in this chapter was a direct one: "Do we need the church?" My answer does not assume that those who are not Christian need the church to achieve eternal salvation. *I would affirm the need for the church community in terms of a body of people who keep alive the memory of Jesus, whom most Christians would affirm is very much alive, though varied individuals might explain or express that differently from how others would, all within the same tradition.*

In keeping with the overall theme of this book, I would also claim that if a particular church community or denomination presents itself in ways that contradict core principles espoused by Jesus, those communities are putting up terrible roadblocks and impeding individuals connected with them from experiencing and living out the heart and soul of the Christian message.

---

6. Jefferson provided his own interpretation of the life of Jesus in this unique, interesting work. This is known as the *Jefferson Bible*.

9

BEFORE WE CONCLUDE . . .

BEFORE WE CONCLUDE THIS BOOK, I want to talk about an important topic which really undergirds this entire book. *I want to talk about God . . .*

This book has explored the *"love hate relationship"* that I have had with the institutional church. Of course, the institutional Christian church is what it is because of its core conviction: *Belief in God made manifest in Jesus of Nazareth, Jesus, whom the church declares as the Christ.* At the heart of Christian faith is that this man Jesus of Nazareth communicates to humanity the living presence of God. *In the well-known creedal document, the conviction is expressed this way:*

"We believe in one Lord, Jesus Christ . . . God from God, light from light . . . "[1]

Now, what is important here for us to take into consideration is this: What do we mean when we find ourselves thinking about and talking about God? Some of you reading this may find this foray into theology somewhat unnecessary. One of the assumptions we make of those who hold to being part of the church is a faith in God. Yet what I contend is that we need to ask this question of one another: *What can you tell me about the God whom you believe in?*

The renowned scholar and writer Marcus Borg spoke and wrote frequently about how he challenged his college students with that question whenever they declared that they either did not believe in or questioned the existence of God. Truth be told, there is most definitely a plethora of

---

1. From The Nicene Creed

answers to that quite complicated question. Before we conclude this book, I want to pause here and do a brief overview of those potential responses. The reason for this is that as we explore any individual relationship we may have with the church (love, hate or in between), we need to recognize that a fair assumption about the church is that its members and those connected to it hold to some kind of a belief in God!

So, then, when we say we believe in God and are asked to spell out what it is that constitutes the essence of our beliefs, what might be our possible responses?

NOT A DIVERSION

I want to make clear at this point that our exploration of different ways of looking at God is not a diversion from the underlying message of this book. While the book *is* about the institution called church and our relationship to it, be it that of love, hate or indifference, it is important to keep in mind that to believer, non-believer and agnostic alike, the significance of the church is connected to one's understanding of God. In addition, we also must recognize that the word church itself came out of Christian scripture and tradition. As we have noted in this book, the word itself refers to the community of people who affirm faith in Jesus of Nazareth and make important claims about who He is!

What is interesting is that even within the body of the church, an institution which makes some significant affirmations about the person Jesus and about God or the divine, there is considerable diversity and variety of thought and belief. It is important therefore to take a little time here and go into some comparative detail about the different ways in which God is understood within the Christian tradition. In doing so, I would also suggest that within the religious education programs of local churches, this issue of God be given significant attention in programs offered to people of all ages. In my book Christian Faith for Adolescents[2], *I recommend that young people be exposed to an in-depth process of thinking about what is involved in thinking about God.* Young people and adults need to be assisted in moving beyond understandings of God that merely reflect doctrinal statements they have been trained to repeat. Oftentimes, these statements of faith strike people as inadequate when they are faced with significant crises and tragedies in

---

2. *Christian Faith for Adolescents, LaRochelle, Energion, 2017*

their lives[3]. Ideally, religious education would serve as a way of helping people deal with the complexities and mysteries inherent in being a human being! Religious education should encourage the individual to embrace experience and intellect alike!

As we conclude this book, let's stop and look at the ways people have developed their ideas about God. My hope is that you, the reader, might give serious thought to where you stand in relation to these varied approaches and understandings. Ideally, it would be great if you could engage in serious conversations with others about this:

A LITERAL UNDERSTANDING OF THE BIBLE

One place from which people get their understanding of God is from specific citations from the Bible. Within the Christian church, the literal understanding of the Bible has a significant influence on individuals. Quite honestly, the usual pattern of exposure to the Bible for those adults who are or have been connected to a church is this: learning Bible stories as a child in Sunday School or whatever structure one's church uses for Christian Education. Wonderful things can happen in Sunday School or in religious education programs for children such as Vacation Bible School and the like. However, what really tends *not* to happen is an in-depth exploration of how the Bible came to be or of some of the built-in challenges and contradictions one might find within it.

What appears therefore to be the predominant approach to biblical texts for people within the pews is a kind of *biblical literalism*. Now, some of this is not problematic in certain contexts. For example, the traditional Christmas stories of angels, a child in a manger, wise men from the East coming to see the child and other well-known stories surrounding the birth of the child provide for many an opportunity to have a significant religious experience around Christmastime every year.

However, what is usually not taught in religious education programs in many, perhaps most, Christian churches is that, while these stories do affirm the event of the birth of Jesus, they contain language and situations that are the stuff of good literature and are not necessarily literal historical descriptions of the events contained within them.

---

3. One of the finest explanations of this may be found in Rabbi Harold Kushner's book *When Bad Things Happen to Good People*.

Before We Conclude . . .

I would suggest that it is this literal understanding of Biblical texts that stands in the way of an understanding of the Bible and consequently of God that makes sense to the inquiring mind, as well as to the individual who seeks to apply convictions inherent in the Christian tradition to the living out of her/his everyday life. Honestly, this is a position that reflects what is found in good Biblical scholarship in Catholic, Protestant and Orthodox traditions. My point is that because of Biblical literalism, it is most likely that one will be unable to come to terms with the depth and significance that lies at the heart of the Christian message. Since this literalism has been the undergirding approach to reading Biblical texts, those who see Scripture through its lens are at a disadvantage in their reading of the Bible and in their interpretation of the relevance of these texts to their contemporary lives.

When a church falls short of offering good, in-depth Biblical study which draws on sources available to pastors and others who have been trained to teach within their congregations, those who are part of the church are deprived of opportunities to explore the books of the Bible in depth. This, in turn, can contribute to a literal understanding of God which falls short of challenging the individual with a more in depth understanding of this complex mystery.

It is extremely important that when members and friends of congregations speak to a pastor or educational leader about what Bible edition they should possess, the response would point these individuals in the direction of a Bible which includes footnotes and introductory writings that emphasize the background regarding how these Biblical texts were composed. Quite frankly, there are many Bible editions out there that do not consider the full range of understanding and interpretations regarding certain Biblical passages. It should be a realistic expectation that a trained clergyperson or member of congregation with an academic background in up-to-date Biblical interpretation can point interested congregants and inquirers in the right direction. In my view, my experience has been that many mainline churches fall short of providing these opportunities locally, as well as opportunities to learn more about the whys in the worship style of that church or denomination.

Within the Bible, one would find a good number of texts that *should* challenge the reader because they offer viewpoints that may very well appear to contradict some of the core beliefs of Christian faith and/or have shaped the formulation of certain Christian doctrines within the churches as these texts have been used to offer proofs for certain teachings of the church.

Here are some examples:

1. I would begin by citing Genesis 1:27–28 which states as that man and woman are to be fruitful and multiply. This has led historically to a position held within some Christian traditions that married couples should be expected to have children. In some traditions, it has even led to a church teaching that a couple should not impede the conception of a child by using any method of birth control. *This scriptural passage has thus become a proof text which backs up a doctrinal position of the church.* This raises the question of original intent. i.e., is this what the passage was intended for as it was passed along by word of mouth and eventually became part of a text known as Genesis 1? In the minds of some, because it is in the Bible, it would therefore be seen as a direct declaration from God. *This interpretation deserves to be challenged and it has been challenged by Biblical scholars within Christianity.* This literal interpretation does not reflect what is taught in the seminaries of mainline Protestantism or in the work of great Catholic Biblical scholars.

One could cite many other challenging examples:

2. Genesis 19:4–5 and Leviticus 18:22: Passages used by many to declare homosexuality immoral.
3. 1 Corinthians 14: 3–4: This passage declares that women should be silent in churches and has been used within Christianity to advocate for a male clergy.
4. 1 Timothy 2:11–12: A Biblical citation stating that women are to keep quiet in church.

I would contend that as church educators and pastors teach about the Bible, it is vital that they spend considerable time and effort challenging the tendency toward simplistic Biblical literalism prevalent within much of institutional Christianity!

One could go on at length and offer troubling quotations that one would find in the Bible, including those that have been used historically to defend racial segregation and slavery. The good news is that there is outstanding Biblical study available within Christianity to those who wish to seek it out. It seems to me that local churches and pastors need to do all they can to provide opportunities. It is important that pastors find a way to introduce those within their churches to sound Biblical scholarship.

THEOLOGY DEVELOPED WITHIN THE INSTITUTIONAL CHURCH

Within the many churches that have emerged within Christianity, one will find a variety of approaches to questions concerning God. Within Roman Catholicism, for example, much of the understanding of God is attributable to the work of Thomas Aquinas. Catholic catechisms have been strongly influenced by his theology. In the definition and explanation of God which has emerged from his work, one sees the divine as described as being omnipresent, omniscient, and omnipotent. These *three omnis* refer to a God who is everywhere, sees all and has ultimate power. In this understanding, God assumes person like qualities of the very highest degree. Some religious traditions advocate for this position from the perspective of natural theology. The work of Thomas Aquinas stands out as exceptionally thorough. In the very first class I walked into in college, a philosophy class, we spent many weeks going into detail regarding proofs for the existence of God. As I have noted previously, I attended a Catholic college, and this course was taught by a Jesuit priest who was highly skilled on his knowledge of what we would call natural theology. In essence, his driving conviction was that built into the human person is an understanding found in Aquinas' works which demonstrates that as we look back at causes for all existence and the existence of human beings, all logical evidence points to a divine presence who got this whole process started. This is found in an understanding of the presence of an unmoved mover.

While Aquinas' position might be defended by many Protestant thinkers, most Protestant thinking regarding God came from the tradition's understanding of the place of the Bible in Christian living. The Protestant emphasis on Biblical teaching as normative led to yet another emphasis, i.e., the recognition that the Bible is not in error. Consequently, in most Protestant preaching, in traditional Protestant theological circles, one would see that Biblical citations are paramount in presenting evidence of what the text is intended to say. Within Protestantism, interpretations of various passages within the Scripture may differ. A classic distinction would be that between traditional Calvinism and the Biblical interpretations of Martin Luther. Yet. despite some fascinating nuances of difference, the fact remains that the process leading to these stated conclusions places high emphasis on the teachings expressed in the sacred books of the Bible. While a traditional Roman Catholic schooled in Aquinas might cite (legitimately) Biblical texts which make the three omnis credible, the methodology of traditional Catholicism is more tilted in favor of the logical proof method that that of strict Biblical proof texting.

It should be noted that within Protestantism, there has been a history of developing catechisms that were to be used for the teaching of children and youth, as well as for those considering membership in Protestant churches. These catechisms included specific doctrinal statements unique to the theology of that tradition that have shaped the thinking of those schooled within them. What is common in the traditional Biblical interpretations found within Catholic, Protestant and Orthodox traditions is an anthropomorphic understanding of God, i.e., attributing person like qualities to the divine. This is the idea that one looks at a person and just makes God larger. One description leans in the direction of projecting God as humanity on a larger scale. Much well-developed theology, while quite orthodox with respect to core Christian teachings, suggests caution with respect to these kinds of anthropomorphic interpretations of God. Here is where I suggest a careful reading of the works of theologians such as Karl Rahner as well as Elizabeth Johnson.

A MORE SPECULATIVE BRAND OF THEOLOGY

While there have been many different influences on Christians and churches throughout the centuries, constant over a period of hundreds of years were the Trinitarian emphases found in the theology of Catholics, Protestants and Orthodox alike, all of which tilted in favor what I describe above, i.e., the emphasis on a God with characteristics people would identify as person like. However, in the 1950's, here in the United States, those who were attending Protestant seminaries and studying religion on their undergraduate campuses, encountered the work found in the writings of varied theologians which called into question the traditionalist teachings as described above. One of these theologians, the renowned Paul Tillich, wrote in considerable detail about a God he described as 'the ground of all being.'[4]' This position drew the distinction between God as person like being and God as the underpinning of all being. Tillich was not alone and much of Protestant theology explored the question of God from this perspective. Within Catholicism, the writings of Pierre Teilhard de Chardin presented a picture of a dynamic God as a force of evolution[5], a position far removed from the emotionless deity often identified within the more traditional proof texts within Catholicism. One sees the influence of Teilhard in the work of John Haught and Ilia Delio, distinguished Roman Catholic theologians in our time.

As years moved along decades back, John Robinson, a renowned bishop/scholar from the Church of England, wrote his groundbreaking work entitled *Honest to God* in which he questioned many of the assumptions of traditional Christian theology, including providing reinterpretations on matters such as the Trinity, the Virgin Birth and more.

Over time, several theologians have emerged who have offered a variety of interpretations of God that have challenged the more traditional understandings. These theologians, often identified with process theology and panentheism often offer some specific, confident explanations of how God operates, with some emphasizing the concept of God's lure. Others, such as Forrest Church, have found themselves comfortable in saying that one cannot really understand God this side of eternity. The scholar Karen Armstrong has presented us with great background and insights into the variety of understandings we human beings have about God. The recently deceased Episcopal bishop and scholar John Shelby Spong has had a significant influence on those who question Biblical literalism and who embrace the concept of mystery in relation to our understanding of God. A close examination of theological writing over the last few decades shows that there has been considerable diversity of theological viewpoints and opinions.

- From the time of the establishment of this country, the religious establishment was comprised of those within Protestant denominations such as Congregationalists, Episcopalians, Methodists, Baptists, and others, with a growing number of Catholics and a vibrant Jewish community.

---

4. This has become a well known phrase in the field of theology.

5. This opened the door to a new understanding of the relationship between theology and science within the Catholic tradition. .

- Within those traditions, contrary to some popular opinion, there have been differences and diversity.
- This diversity has led to divergent approaches within many religious traditions. For example, there are those who self-identify as Christians or Jews who would hold to their belief in a personal God with maximized characteristics of a human being. For others, their beliefs would be closer to a panentheistic understanding.

As for me:

1. *I believe in God though I cannot state definitively what God might look like.*
2. *I believe in God even though I cannot claim to have an infallible handle on explaining exactly how God works in this world or why a God allows certain things to happen . . . or whether it is even a question of God's allowing.*
3. *Ultimately, I am OK with mystery primarily because I place faith that the mystery in which I believe is a loving mystery.*

With the theologian Karl Rahner whose work I find fascinating, even with all its complications, I would affirm as well that this loving mystery is expressed in the person of Jesus of Nazareth, the One we call *'the Christ'*. I am also fascinated by some of the theological writing which points to a suffering God. I am struck by Elie Wiesel's insights about the Holocaust in his amazing work, *Night* in particular, this powerful passage:

> *Then came the march past the victims. The two men were no longer alive. Their tongues were hanging out, swollen and bluish. But the third rope was still moving: the child, too light, was still breathing . . . And so he remained for more than half an hour, lingering between life and death, writhing before our eyes. And we were forced to look at him at close range. He was still alive when I passed him. His tongue was still red, his eyes not yet extinguished. Behind me, I heard the same man asking: "For God's sake, where is God?" And from within me, I heard a voice answer "Where is He? This is where – hanging here from these gallows . . . "*[6]

None of this is to say that God cannot be in our lives if we do not make certain specific theological affirmations. One need not ascribe certainty to all the tenets of a particular religious faith to achieve peace and salvation.

6. Elie Wiesel, *Night*.

Before We Conclude . . .

Nor does one need to pretend to know all the answers to this mystery, but, even in the unknowing, can recognize that there is credibility present in this affirmation of faith in the loving mystery. While holding to a faith in a God who is mysterious and in so many ways incomprehensible, I, at the same time, recognize that I (and we) do "walk by faith and not by sight."[7] People interpret that phrase differently with some using it to claim exactitude in what they believe and others embracing the mystery. I tend toward the mystery, all the while trusting and believing that it is a loving mystery!

The bottom line is this: While this side of eternity, we cannot give all the details of life's origins and destiny, one *can* affirm in faith that there is meaning, purpose and ultimate importance found in this reality called life. From my perspective, I will gladly affirm a faith in a God about whom I cannot claim to have all the details or to know all of the answers, a God at the heart of my life, the very pulse of all of creation, present at its beginning, never to depart, in some ways completely incomprehensible, in others, a glorious mystery, a mystery imbued with a truly amazing grace!

---

7. 2 Corinthians:5–7

10

In Conclusion

As we move to the conclusion of this book, there are some observations I would like to share, In fact, in the ideal world, I am hoping that what I state below will form the basis for some conversations you will have. Perhaps these conversations will be with people in your church community or maybe they will be about church with those both connected and skeptical. These observations are inspired by events within the realm of church at the time of this writing. Some of them reflect trends that have been on the rise over these past few decades. I hope you find them helpful or at least worthy of serious thought and conversation:

1. *The reality is that over these last few decades, we have seen significant decline in worship attendance, particularly within the mainline churches.*

2. *Over this time, there has been a great increase in the number of people who refer to themselves as nones, i.e. those without formal religious affiliation.*

3. *Over these past few decades, there has been growth in the "progressive movement" within Christianity. This movement's appeal, however, has been primarily to those of advanced educational backgrounds.*

4. *There has been considerable growth in conservative, non-denominational churches.*

5. *There has been an emergence of energy and scholarship in many mainline Protestant denominations and in varied pockets of Catholicism.*

In Conclusion

Nonetheless, in both Catholicism and Protestantism, the more conservative elements are dominant.

Before I sat down to finalize this book, I had to deal with a battle within myself. In short, I found myself in a struggle about what to title this book. Originally, I opted for A Love-Hate Relationship, a title which I felt accurately described my experience with the institutional church. As I proceeded to engage in writing the book, it became quite clear to me that the title did not capture the essence of what I was trying to say. Up until the time I made the decision to title this *I Love the Church, I Hate the Church*, I must confess that I struggled with the title! As I thought about it even further, I decided that it was important to add the question: *Paradox or Contradiction?* to the title, finding this expressive of the kinds of questions I have intended to raise for those who would read this book!

The reason for this inner battle was simple: In my life, this institution called church has been extremely important. Many of its leaders have influenced me. Its institutions have provided me a wonderful education and opportunities to explore the deepest questions humanity faces. I look back at my years as an altar boy, religion teacher and clergyperson within the institutional church with a great deal of joy. *In a very real sense, this does not appear to the stuff of which hate is made.*

However, on the other hand, as you have read, there are customs and traditions I have found within the institutional church that trouble me and what bothers me most within institutional Christianity is what Jesus alludes to in when He says: *'You disregard the values of God and 'cling to human tradition.'*[1]

It is that tension between the life and teachings of Jesus and the way that Christianity is taught within the institutional church that has driven me to write this book. In writing this, I do so fully aware of my own imperfections and that I, as with all of humanity, "fall short of the glory of God"[2]. I do not write this from the perspective of a perfect human being criticizing the 'Body of Christ', a popular title describing the heart and soul of the institutional church. Instead, I write this as part of an institution which seeks to espouse, teach, and live out the teachings of Jesus and oftentimes falls quite short.

---

1. Mark 7:8
2. Romans 3:23

I Love the Church, I Hate the Church

Many, many times, in my experience as an ordained clergyperson within churches in both Catholic and Protestant tradition, I have sat at meetings or participated in conversations where I have found myself asking the question: '*What does any of this have to do with trying to live out the message of Jesus?*' In stating this, I, at the same time, want to acknowledge all of the hard working people in churches I have served who have poured heart, soul and energy into pancake breakfasts, spaghetti suppers, tag sales and the like, all intended to raise money for the church for the wonderful reason that through these funds the church can do its work, i.e. the church can find ways to reach out to the needy and provide help to families who need it.

At the same time, I have also found myself frustrated by conversations at church meetings about parking lots, roofs and the like, often concerned that the money a church may allocate in those areas could best be used to take care of the poor[3]. I have worried about what I have perceived to be a misplaced focus. I have often asked myself and others the question: What has any of this concern got to do with Jesus, the one who literally *took to the streets* to get out the message He sought to teach?

In asking these questions, I could not escape two realities within me that I continue to hold in tension:

1. *Yes, I do love the church in which I was nourished, sustained and blessed to serve. I cherish the people I know and have known who were and are part of this community of faith.*

2. *Yes, I also despise the many ways in which this institution called church has fallen so short of the intentions expressed in the Gospel. I am troubled by the aberrations embraced by right wing Christianity and the ways many churches have focused on an approach to religion which misses the mark when it comes to prioritizing the message and the life of Jesus.*

In sharing this internal struggle with you, as one who has lived his life within the institution, I draw strength and inspiration from those in the church who have inspired me throughout the years. It is interesting how, despite my many criticisms of 'organized Christianity', I look back on my life and think of those Christian individuals, both publicly known and known to me because their lives somehow intersected with mine, people like Cesar Chavez, Dietrich Bonhoeffer, Dorothy Day, Dan Berrigan, William Sloane Coffin, Jean Donovan and many, many more I have come to

---

3. I recommend Mark 10:21 as a good illustration of this.

In Conclusion

know in the churches I have served and the places I have worked, people who have been part of this community called church who understood that *when all is said and done, it's not about rules, specific dogmas, policies, procedures or ritual. Instead, they have shown that, when all is said and done, when push comes to shove, it is really all about Jesus.*

Because of them, despite the anger I have felt when the institution has veered away from its ideals . . . Because of them, in spite of the hatred I acknowledge when this institution that has shaped my life has gone off the rails . . . Because of them, I have to say . . . way down deep, despite the anger, disillusion and discouragement I have often found . . . Because of them, I can't deny it . . . *Despite all of the things over the years that I have found discouraging and contrary to what the church is really meant to be, all those things I have learned to despise and outright hate, the simple fact remains: Yes, way down deep, when all is said and done, despite all that along the way I have learned to despise and hate, when all is said and done . . . YES . . . I really do love the church!'*.

Bibliography

Borg, Marcus. *Speaking Christian: Why Christian Words Have Lost Their Meaning and Power—And How They Can Be Restored*. San Francisco: HarperOne, 2011.

Burge, Ryan. *The Nones: Where They Came From, Who They Are, and Where They Are Going*. Minneapolis: Fortress, 2021.

Carroll, James. *Christ Actually: Reimagining Faith in the Modern Age*. New York: Penguin, 2014.

Kavanaugh, James. *A Modern Priest Looks at His Outdated Church*. New York: Trident, 1967.

LaRochelle, Robert. *Crossing the Street*. Gonzalez ,FL: Energion, 2012.

McBrien, Richard. *Do We Need the Church?* New York: HarperCollins, 1969.

Niebuhr, H. Richard. *Christ and Culture*. New York: Harper & Row, 1951.

www.ingramcontent.com/pod-product-compliance
Lightning Source LLC
Chambersburg PA
CBHW070918160426
43193CB00011B/1507